CLAIMS IN CONFLICT

CLAIMS IN CONFLICT

Retrieving and Renewing the Catholic Human Rights Tradition

by
David Hollenbach, S.J.

PAULIST PRESS
New York/Ramsey/Toronto

Library of Congress
Catalog Card Number: 79-84239

ISBN: 0-8091-2197-2 (paper)
ISBN: 0-8091-0287-0 (cloth)

Published by Paulist Press
Editorial Office: 1865 Broadway, New York, N.Y. 10023
Business Office: 545 Island Road, Ramsey, N.J. 07446

Printed and bound in the
United States of America

Contents

To my mother and father,
brothers and sister,
who know the meaning of
love and justice.

Preface

During the past several years the topic of human rights has moved to the center of moral and political debate. This book has been written out of a conviction that Roman Catholic thought has something important to contribute to this debate and also something important to learn from it.

Looked at internationally, the Catholic Church has become one of the most visible non-governmental actors in the struggle for human rights. At the base of this action lies the one hundred year tradition of modern Catholic social thought, a tradition which began when Leo XIII became Pope in 1878 and which continues to develop today. Catholic social thought has been formulated in the language of rights throughout this period. The theoretical sophistication with which the tradition has addressed a wide array of human rights issues has given it both conceptual strength and practical suppleness. In a debate where confusion and rigidity often seem ironically linked, Catholic thought may prove an important resource for all participants.

At the same time the pluralism of basic moral and political perspectives which is so evident in a forum like the United Nations does not fit easily in the Catholic moral universe. Uneasiness with disagreement and the desire for a minimum of conflict has often blunted the practical contribution of the Catholic community to the defense of human rights.

This book, then, is an effort at critical appropriation and sympathetic criticism. It focuses on those aspects of the human rights struggle which are most important in the relations between nations, especially between rich nations and poor ones. The economic rights of the poor and the political rights of those living under authoritarian regimes are currently more honored in rhetoric than in reality. Increasing the level of genuine respect for these rights will call for significant changes in the advanced industrial nations of the West. Both the strengths of the Catholic tradition which are emphasized and the weaknesses which are criticized are those which appear most important in this framework. Other "rights issues" are hotly debated today, for example, the rights of the sick and the dying, the rights of women, the right to life, etc. These are evidently in need of serious reflection and analysis, especially in the Catholic community. Nonetheless, the importance of the questions which arise in the transnational context seem to me to justify the book's focus.

The late John Courtney Murray's magisterial work on the right of religious freedom has served as inspiration and model throughout the writing of this book. Within the American context, Murray forged a theoretical foundation for religious liberty which helped America and Catholicism learn from each other. My effort to retrieve and renew Catholic thought on the whole constellation of human rights in an international context is a modest effort to carry Murray's work a step further. It is part of a larger project underway at the Woodstock Theological Center on the topic "Human Rights, Needs and Power in an Interdependent World." The Center is examining the political and economic context of the human rights debate, the normative foundations of the human rights theory and potential ways of improving the implementation of human rights. A number of questions which are left unexplored here will be dealt with more thoroughly in further studies by the Center staff. But, I am, of course, responsible for the limits of what I have written.

Many persons have inspired, stimulated, aided and criticized my analysis and conclusions. The Woodstock Theological Center has provided support during two summers of research and writing. The Center staff has read and criticized various drafts along the way. I especially want to thank Robert Mitchell, Brian Smith, John Langan, Drew Christiansen, John Haughey, Thomas Clarke, Margaret Crahan and José Zalaquett for their constantly helpful support. William Ryan, Peter Henriot, Philip Land and Joe Holland of the Center of Concern have provided challenging comments on a number of occasions. The initial research and an earlier version of Chapters II, III, and IV were part of a dissertation written at Yale University. Charles Powers and Margaret Farley were of enormous intellectual and personal assistance during that phase of the project. My colleagues and students at Weston School of Theology and the Boston Theological Institute have provided much encouragement. Alice Halsema, Betty Mullen, Mary Street and Arlene Sullivan typed and retyped the manuscript. I am grateful to them for their patience. Finally, I want to thank my brother Jesuits, especially those who have shared my hopes and frustrations in our common call to translate Christian faith into action for justice.

David Hollenbach, S.J.
Weston School of Theology
Cambridge, Massachusetts

Part One
Context

Chapter One
The Human Rights Debate

The political debate in the United States on the relation between morality and public policy is at a critical turning point.

A new language can be heard in presidential addresses, on the floor of the Congress, in the manifestos of minorities and women and around the conference tables of international negotiations. It is the language of human rights. The vocabulary of this language is crisp, blunt, almost curt. Human beings have rights. These rights are to be respected. Ronald Dworkin has captured the tone of the rights vocabulary by calling rights "political trumps held by individuals." [1] If a claimed right is truly a right there can, it seems, be neither legal nor moral appeal against it. The simple fact that someone makes a claim, however, does not mean that that claim must be respected. Claims often conflict. Some of them are incompatible with others. People sometimes make impossible, illegal, even immoral claims and occasionally they use the language of rights when they do. The determination of which claims are justified and therefore qualify as human rights is a crucial task.[2] The clarity of the rights vocabulary is far from being matched by our understanding of what human rights are, how they are interrelated, how they are limited by each other, and whether they can ever be subordinated to other social values.

That claims to be entitled to certain things by right are being taken with a new seriousness is evident from several recent political developments. In a major address before the General Assembly of the United Nations in 1977, President Jimmy Carter affirmed in challenging tones that worldwide respect for the political and economic rights of all people was to be a cornerstone of his foreign policy. He told the delegates:

> The search for peace and justice also means respect for human dignity. All the signatories of the U.N. Charter have pledged themselves to observe and to respect basic human rights. Thus, no member of the United Nations can claim that mistreatment of its own citizens is solely its own business. Equally, no member can avoid its responsibilities to review and to speak when torture or unwarranted deprivation occurs in any part of the world.[3]

This same note of urgency has been translated into action by Congressional restrictions placed on U.S. military and economic aid to governments which use torture, arbitrary arrest or systematic discrimination as political tools. In two votes, in 1975 and 1976, the Congress outlawed foreign aid, both military and economic, to "any country which engages in a consistent pattern of gross violations of internationally recognized human rights" "unless such aid directly benefits the needy." The same Congress also acknowledged that all persons possess a "right to food" which is to be respected by U.S. economic and agricultural policy. The 1975 Helsinki Conference on Security and Cooperation in Europe, in its Final Act, declared that the nations of the North Atlantic and Eastern Europe, including the United States and the Soviet Union, have agreed to respect "freedom of thought, conscience, religion or belief without distinction as to race, sex, language or religion." [4] This same treaty also pledged respect for all the economic and social rights "which derive from the inherent dignity of the human person and are essential for his free and full development." [5] The Helsinki Accords specified mechanisms for international review of the implementation of these commitments by the signatory nations.

Perhaps the most far-reaching indication of the emergence of concern for human rights as a serious policy issue in the United States was the pledge made by President Carter in his U.N. address. He announced his intention to seek ratification of two United Nations covenants on human rights—the International Covenant on Economic, Social, and Cultural Rights and the International Covenant on Civil and Political Rights. In 1948 the United States voted for the Universal Declaration of Human

Rights in the U.N. General Assembly. This Declaration is not, however, a binding treaty subject to the full strictures of international law. The Declaration was to serve as a "standard of achievement"[6] for the nations of the world, not as a binding legal document. The two Covenants, on the other hand, have the legal force of binding treaties for those nations which have ratified them. There has been significant resistance in the United States during the past thirty years to acceptance of such international obligations as unwise restrictions on U.S. national sovereignty.[7]

Ratification of the Covenant on Economic, Social and Cultural Rights would commit the United States to the protection of such rights by "taking steps individually and through international cooperation, especially economic and technical, to the maximum of its available resources . . . including particularly the adoption of legislative measures" [Art. 2]. Among the economic, social and cultural rights specified by this covenant are the following:

— "the right of everyone to an adequate standard of living for himself and his family, including adequate food, clothing and housing" [Art. 11].
— "the right of everyone to form trade unions and to join the trade union of his choice" [Art. 8].
— "the right of everyone to social security, including social insurance" [Art. 9].
— "the fundamental right of everyone to be free from hunger" [Art. 11].
— "the right of everyone to the enjoyment of the highest attainable standard of physical and mental health" [Art. 12]
— "the right of everyone to education" [Art. 13].

This Covenant, if taken seriously, would move the United States toward major new initiatives in international economic policy. The most obvious consequence of ratification would be the public commitment by the United States to major efforts designed to meet the basic economic needs of the poor of the world. Similarly, ratification would make the economic policies of other nations an important concern of U.S. foreign policy and diplomacy. Ratification, therefore, would immediately dispel the false sense that the clarity of rights language provides an easy and righteous escape from either the suffering or social complexity of such problems as world hunger, population growth, and resource scarcity.

The Covenant on Civil and Political Rights is intimately linked with equally complex foreign policy and diplomatic issues. Ratification will put the force of U.S. and international law behind the following statements:

— "Every human being has the inherent right to life . . . No one shall be arbitrarily deprived of his life" [Art. 6].
— "No one shall be subjected to torture or to cruel, inhuman or degrading treatment or punishment" [Art. 7].
— "Everyone has the right to liberty and security of person. No one shall be subject to arbitrary arrest or detention" [Art. 9].
— "Everyone shall be free to leave any country, including his own." This right "shall not be subject to any restrictions except those which are provided by law, (or) are necessary to protect national security" [Art. 12].
— "Everyone shall have the right to freedom of thought, conscience and religion" [Art. 18].
— "Any advocacy of national, racial or religious hatred that constitutes incitement to discrimination, hostility or violence shall be prohibited by law" [Art. 20].

These selections from the two Covenants indicate that Carter's statement and other recent human rights actions have launched the United States into extremely turbulent waters. The achievement of international protection and respect for the rights enumerated here calls for nothing less than the reorganization of both the international economic order and the political relations among nation states. In particular, active support for these two Covenants calls on the United States to adopt both domestic and international economic policies which are designed to redress the economic inequalities which make it impossible for vast numbers of people to obtain "adequate food, clothing and housing" or even to dream of attaining "the highest attainable standard of physical and mental health." Efforts to support the substance of these Covenants have already injected matters of internal political structure and policy such as freedom of speech, religion, emigration and due process into international diplomacy. Ratification will carry this process still further.

The appeal to human rights holds out the promise of great potential benefits to many millions of people around the globe. It also presents the specter of increasing international tension and conflict. In a world where hunger, torture, violation of conscience and potential nuclear conflict are intertwined in a complex network of economic, political and military relations, the need for careful examination of the appropriate ways to play the human rights "trump card" is painfully evident.

One way to keep the heady rhetoric of the human rights debate within the boundaries of prudence and political reality is to regard it as just that—rhetoric. Rights language is frequently the language of protest, of the manifesto and of the political broadside. The appeal to rights has a flamboyance and volatility which make its use especially congenial in political conflict, whether by persons seeking to protest ways in which they are being wronged or by those seeking to protect their own special interests. Nations, too, find the discussion of their goals and interests in terms of rights to be of great ideological advantage. Consequently rights claims have a natural tendency to expand over ever greater ranges of the moral and political landscape. This expansionism has been described critically by Iredell Jenkins in a discussion of the renewed emphasis on human rights which has been notable in political discourse since the Second World War:

> There is much in the doctrine of human rights that deserves the sympathy and support of all men. There is so much unnecessary suffering and wanton abuse and neglect of men in need that a doctrine that cries out against these conditions and demands their correction merits both our thanks and our attention. . . . But there is also much in this doctrine that seems unsound and imbalanced, arousing doubts and reservations in the minds of many. . . . The doctrine seems altogether devoid of internal restraints and controls. It is a dangerous doctrine because it advances no criteria, whether theoretical, empirical or practical, for determining its reach.

> It grounds rights in humanity, and then leaves the notion undefined, so that the content of rights is indefinite and indeterminate.[8]

If, as Jenkins suggests, our understanding of what human rights are is without theoretical control then the current debate must indeed be regarded as an ideological or rhetorical cloak for other political concerns. These concerns, such as the elimination of torture or hunger are of the greatest human importance and moral urgency. But unless it can be shown that both such claims can and must be met, the language of rights begins to dissolve into what Jeremy Bentham called "nonsense—nonsense on stilts." [9] For, in Bentham's cutting words, "a reason for wishing that a certain right were established, is not that right—want is not supply—hunger is not bread."[10] It is clear that neither the right not to be tortured nor the right to be free from hunger is established in many parts of the world. The question then, is whether it can be shown that both these rights ought to be established and that this can, in fact, be done in the world we live in.

The attempt to answer this question involves a threefold task. First, the foundation or ground of the general concept of rights must be determined. Second, it must be established how various human rights are related to each other and whether there can ever be a legitimate "trade off" between a particular right and either other rights or other social values. Finally, the relation between human rights as moral claims and the institutions of social, economic and political life must be explored.

The subsequent chapters of this book will examine the ways in which modern Roman Catholic social thought has approached these questions of the ground, interrelation and institutionalization of human rights. The approaches taken by the Catholic tradition to these three basic issues are tightly interwoven with each other and often difficult to analyze separately. It will be useful to prepare the way for an analysis of this tradition by briefly considering several other contemporary ways of thinking about human rights. Such an exploration will help make clearer the distinctiveness of the Roman Catholic approach. The tradition's strengths and possible usefulness will be brought out if we approach it within this larger context. It will also help clarify the weaknesses and possible dangers of the Roman Catholic rights theory.

The three contemporary schools of political thought and action we will consider as the context for an analysis of the Roman Catholic tradition are liberal democracy, Marxism, and the human rights pronouncements of the United Nations.[11] The contrasts between these traditions illuminate some of the major points of disagreement in the current human rights debate. The three traditions are also major ideological and political contenders in the present international arena.[12]

Liberal Democracy

The Bill of Rights of the United States Constitution and the Declaration of the Rights of Man and Citizen of the French Revolution were both intellectual shots heard 'round the political world. They inaugurated the liberal theory of rights in its modern form.[13] The first ten amendments to the American Constitution continue as the human rights charter of modern liberal democracy. The rights to freedom of religion, speech and assembly, the right to be secure in one's person and property, and the rights of *habeas corpus* and to due process of law are defining characteristics of the liberal democratic state. They are rights denied in many parts of the world today, in authoritarian regimes of the right and in totalitarian regimes of the left. The religious freedom of Christians and Jews is restricted in the Soviet Union. Torture and summary imprisonment are used against political dissidents in Indonesia, Uganda and El Salvador. Any semblance of true political participation is denied to blacks in South Africa.

The rights set forth in the liberal theory are related to each other by their common foundation in the freedom of the individual person. To attack or restrict these fundamental rights is to attack individual liberty, the most precious of human values in liberal thought. For John Locke, one of the fathers of the liberal rights doctrine, the natural state of humanity is the foundation of all legitimate political power. This is a state in which all persons possess

> perfect freedom to order their actions, and dispose of their possessions and persons, as they see fit, within the bounds of the law of nature, without asking leave, or depending upon the will of any other man.[14]

Professor H. L. A. Hart has stated the moral foundation which undergirds this political theory most succinctly. He has argued that if there are any rights at all they are ramifications and extrapolations of individual freedom. In Hart's view not only constitutionally guaranteed legal rights but those moral rights which legitimate them are rooted in the fundamental right to liberty. Hart's thesis is a trenchant summary of the prevailing interpretation of both the liberal theory and the liberal experience. It runs as follows:

> If there are any moral rights at all, it follows that there is at least one natural right, the equal right of all to be free. By saying that there is this right, I mean that in the absence of certain special conditions which are consistent with the right being an equal right, any adult human being capable of choice (1) has the right to forbearance on the part of all others from the use of coercion or restraint against him save to hinder coercion or restraint and (2) is at liberty to do (i.e., is under no obligation to abstain from) any action which is not one coercing or restraining or designed to injure other persons.[15]

For Hart, then, rights are negative. They are defenses of individual liberty. They are immunities from interference by others, claims to "forbearance on the part of all others." Rights are the fences around that field where the individual may act, speak, worship, associate or accumulate wealth without restriction by the positive action of either other persons or the state. The location of the perimeter of this field of freedom is also determined negatively. There are duties corresponding to rights in this theory, but they are negative rather than positive in content. Any action is protected by right "which is not one coercing or restraining or designed to injure other persons." This requirement excludes preventing others from doing what they choose unless these others are themselves attacking liberty. It excludes attempts to restrict the liberty of others by force or the threat of force. It rules out all killing (except in self defense). It outlaws slavery. As Hart notes, however, the liberal theory does not exclude competition, "even though in fact, owing to scarcity, one man's satisfaction causes another's frustration." [16]

It is this last conclusion which has opened the liberal rights theory to serious criticism from the left. C. B. Macpherson's studies of the origin of liberalism in the writings of Hobbes and Locke have pointed out an important affinity between the eighteenth-century rights theory and the emergent market economy of the time. The classical and medieval theorists of natural law insisted upon the reality of positive duties toward others within a stable social order. In rejecting this tradition, liberalism cut the moral cords which tied men and women to the remnants of the disintegrating feudal order. It set them free to participate in the modern capitalist enterprise. As Macpherson puts it, early liberalism "put every man on his own in a market society." [17] In the view of Isaiah Berlin, this link between the liberal rights theory and the legitimacy of unlimited competition and acquisition of wealth "troubles the consciences of Western liberals." [18] Hart is aware that "it will be pedantic to point out to [the poor] that though they are starving they are free." [19] Despite their uneasiness, however, neither Hart nor Berlin is willing to modify his commitment to negative freedom and defensive rights as the basis of democratic politics. Thus, it would seem, the liberal rights theory is compatible with the presence of extreme want in a society, even when the resources necessary to eliminate it are present.

Several representatives of the liberal tradition have recently argued that the theory need not be as ruthless in its economic consequences as the criticisms from the left suggest it must be. For example, John Chapman has suggested that Locke's defense of unlimited liberty to accumulate wealth can be construed as a defense of the value of economic competition for society as a whole. The increased productivity stimulated by competition will, or should, benefit not only the wealthy but the poor as well. Thus Chapman believes that Locke, and the liberal tradition after him, "has accepted the optimum conditions implied in the concept of economic rationality."[20] Chapman's argument in favor of the humaneness of liberal rights theory is a familiar one in contemporary U.S. discussions of economic rights. It turns on two presuppositions, one normative and the other empirical.

The normative presupposition has been stated best by the American philosopher John Rawls. Rawls' masterful elaboration and reconstruction of the liberal tradition is built on what he calls a "general conception" of justice. This conception is a normative standard for determining which inequalities in society are justified and which are not. Rawls formulates his standard this way:

> All social primary goods—liberty and opportunity, income and wealth, and the bases of self-respect—are to be distributed equally unless an unequal distribution of any or all of these goods is to the advantage of the least favored.[21]

Chapman accepts this normative standard. He believes that it represents the moral core of the liberal theory of rights, namely the conviction that "all should benefit, absolutely at least, from inequality in any form." [22] He thinks that it is at least possible to interpret the Lockean and liberal theory of liberty in accordance with this principle. If it can be shown that competition and economic freedom will benefit all, including the least advantaged, then the fact that freedom creates inequality does not count against the liberal theory. The hypothesis that this has been shown is Chapman's second presupposition. The question of its truth is an empirical rather than a normative one.

In *A Theory of Justice* Rawls makes clear that he recognizes the distinction between the defense of liberty and the effort to insure that no one benefits at the expense of another. Rawls' general conception of justice, and the theory of rights it implies, is subdivided into two principles. Simplifying his formulation somewhat, the principles read as follows:

First Principle

> Each person is to have an equal right to the most extensive total system of basic liberties compatible with a similar system of liberty for all.

Second Principle

> Social and economic inequalities are to be arranged so that they are both: (a) to the greatest benefit of the least advantaged . . ., and (b) attached to offices and positions open to all under conditions of fair equality of opportunity.[23]

In Rawls' theory the two principles of justice are not of equal weight. They are ordered "lexically." A lexical order is one "which requires us to satisfy the first principle in the ordering before we move on to the second. . . . A principle does not come into play until those previous to it are either fully met or do not apply." [24] Thus the First Principle, the principle of equal liberty, has an "absolute weight" relative to the principle which calls for basic societal structures designed to benefit the least advantaged. "Liberty can be restricted only for the sake of liberty." [25] The basic liberties which the First Principle defends are the fundamental rights of liberal democracy: political liberty, including the right to vote and be elected to office, freedom of speech and assembly, freedom of conscience and of thought, freedom to hold personal property, and freedom from arbitrary arrest and seizure.[26] Rawls thinks that this ordering should not be objectionable to the poor or those who are otherwise disadvantaged because they are guaranteed the same liberty as the well off, by the First Principle. At the same time the Second Principle assures them that whatever inequalities exist in the economic sphere will be to their benefit, thanks to increased productivity, efficiency or some such mechanism. In other words, in Rawls' version of liberalism the question of satisfying social and economic needs arises only *after* the basic liberal rights have been secured. There can be no trade off between the right of liberty and such rights as the right to food or housing or work. If push should come to shove it would appear that social and economic claims are not rights at all.

Can Rawls reconcile this trade off with his "basic conception" of justice? Can he coherently maintain the priority of liberty and still defend the view that the goods of liberty, opportunity, income, wealth and self-respect are to be equally distributed unless inequalities are to the benefit of those at the bottom? Unfortunately he does not address this question directly. It would appear that a major supposition of the modern liberal tradition makes the question unanswerable. This is the supposition that the goals men and women pursue in their lives—their fundamental conception of what is good—are radically diverse and pluralistic. The individual person has no rational way to judge between those visions of the good life which compete for his or her commitment.[27] Values are options one makes. Since different persons make different options, society is inevitably pluralistic. Because of this plurality of interpretations of what is good and about how a good society should be structured, the value of freedom is preeminent. As Isaiah Berlin has put it:

> Indeed, it is because this is their situation that men place such immense value upon the freedom to choose; for if they had assurance that in some perfect state, realizable by men on earth, no ends pursued by them would ever conflict, the necessity and agony of choice would disappear, and with it the central importance of the freedom to choose.[28]

Berlin recognizes that many of the most powerful and just public movements of our time are built on commitments to positive values other than the value of individual freedom. Thus he acknowledges that the primacy given to the negative right of liberty by liberal thought is no panacea for the conflicts and tragedies that riddle modern society. It is the lack of a rational standard by which to judge between the movements which compete for personal loyalty and social primacy that makes the option for the priority of liberty the safer option in the eyes of the liberal tradition. Since the alternatives to this option are thought to be arbitrary, efforts to impose them on a society smack of tyranny and totalitarianism. To quote Berlin once again:

> Pluralism, with the measure of "negative" liberty that it entails, seems to me a truer and more humane ideal than the

> goals of those who seek in the great, disciplined authoritarian structures the ideal of "positive" self-mastery by classes, or peoples, or the whole of mankind.[29]

The root of the primacy of liberty, therefore, is the conviction that in fact we cannot know in any detail what is truly the good for individual persons. Even less can we know how to institutionalize this good in society. The only humane system of social institutions will be one in which the many values other than liberty are pursued in a way which continues to protect liberty and its "lexical" priority.

The question, then, is this: Is it true that we know as little about the validity of commitments to values other than individual liberty and the means for institutionalizing them as this reading of the liberal theory suggests? On this point Rawls is ambivalent. Rawls believes that we are not totally in the dark about these goods. The general conception of justice calls for an equal distribution of "primary social goods" unless inequality will benefit those who are worst off. Primary goods, according to Rawls' definition, are "things which it is supposed a rational man wants whatever else he wants." [30] They include liberty, opportunity, income, wealth and the bases of self-respect. These goods are the content of a conception of the good which should be rationally acceptable in even a highly pluralistic society. They should also seem reasonable to those in very different types of societies, for example, both to those living in advanced industrial societies and those in societies near or below the level of subsistence. Thus Rawls' general conception of justice appears to call for distributing these primary goods within societies and between societies in such a way that the least advantaged will benefit. A trade off between individual liberty and other social goods seems permissable by the general conception of justice in at least some social situations. Rawls himself admits this, for he acknowledges that the priority of liberty can be limited "if it is necessary to raise the level of civilization" to the point where basic needs have been generally met and where individual liberty can reasonably be called the primary value.[31] This tension within Rawls' theory reveals a fundamental problem facing the liberal theory of rights in our time. On the one hand, the pluralism of cultures, world views and religions makes the defense of liberty an urgent and central concern. The resistance offered to restrictions of civil and political rights provides strong evidence for the reality of this concern. At the same time, the pluralism or inequality in levels of economic development makes inescapable the question of the legitimacy of restricting the economic liberty of the rich in the interests of those in extreme deprivation. Rawls' theory, and the liberal tradition it so persuasively and compassionately represents, does not have an answer for this fundamental problem. It escapes the dilemma by restricting its concern to problems of justice and human rights which arise in societies which are relatively well off. This restriction makes even Rawls' version of the liberal theory of rights an inadequate foundation for developing a human rights policy for our world.

SOVIET MARXISM

Liberal Democratic theory has been vigorously criticized by Marxism for its attempt to separate political freedom from its economic, social and cultural foundations. Hart is prepared to admit that it may be "pedantic" to point out to a starving person that he or she is politically free to eat whatever food can be earned. Rawls is willing to acknowledge that the provisions of a system of equal civil liberties will be of less value to the poor even though these liberties remain real.[32] Marxists, however, regard such statements as hypocritical and cynical. The Marxist tradition rejects Rawls' effort to justify the division of the general conception of justice into two principles, one governing the sphere of civil and political freedoms and the other governing the distribution of wealth, economic opportunity and social participation. Where the liberal democratic rights theory grants primacy to the individual's negative immunity from interference or political coercion, Marxist discussion of human rights stresses positive entitlements to participate fully in the public life of society. Social and economic rights such as the rights to work and material security are preeminent in Marxist theories of rights.

The inseparability of personal freedom and social solidarity is the cornerstone of Marxist social philosophy. Individual and social freedoms can only be realized if they are realized together. Thus political and economic rights are correlative. The goal of Marxism is the creation of a society which has the form of "an association in which the free development of each is the condition for the free development of all." [33] In commenting on the new constitution of the Soviet Union, Leonid Brezhnev affirmed that these words from the Communist Manifesto "have become in practice the fundamental principle of our state." [34]

The centrality of socio-economic rights for Marxism is evident in the new Soviet constitution, as it was in the earlier constitutions of 1918 and 1936. This document guarantees to Soviet citizens the right to work and to choose professions and jobs (with due account of social needs). It proclaims the right to material security, including the right to protection of health. It guarantees the rights to education and housing.[35] It also includes the civil and political rights characteristic of Western democratic constitutionalism: the right to participate in running state and public affairs and the rights to freedom of expression, assembly and the press. The interpretation given to civil and political rights in Communist nations, however, is markedly different from that found in Western democracies.[36]

The chief source of this difference in interpretation is the Marxist conviction that genuine freedom is a social reality. It cannot be achieved by a person acting as an isolated monad but only in solidarity with others. For this reason Marx regarded the rights affirmed by the eighteenth-century authors of the liberal tradition as essentially egoistic. These rights lead "every man to see in other men, not the *realization,* but rather *limitation* of his own liberty." [37] Genuine human liberation or emancipation demands a transformation of the entire social and economic system. Society in all its dimensions must become a living expression and realization of human freedom. In Marx's words:

> Such a transformation will occur only when each person as an individual man, in his everyday life, in his work, and in his relationships . . . has become a *species being;* and when

> he has recognized and organized his own powers *(forces propres)* as *social* powers.[38]

Because civil and political rights ignore this fuller sphere of freedom Marx regarded them as abstractions. The "bourgeois" rights of the individual over against society are reflections of the failure of society to achieve concrete freedom. Equality of political rights denies the relevance of distinctions of birth, social rank, education and occupation for the exercise of freedom in the political sphere. Such equality is abstract, however, because it does not abolish the unequal distribution of power in economic and social life. Equality of civil and political liberties can coexist with the inequality of social and economic classes. The actual fate of freedom in liberal democracy continues to reflect class distinctions in wealth, education and talent. Unequal freedom will continue to be the concrete fact in social life until the inequality of different social classes is abolished. Thus all *real* rights, in Marx's view, are rooted in claims to social and economic equality and only secondarily in claims to political equality. In his words, "Right can never be higher than the economic structure of society and the cultural development conditioned by it." [39]

The goal of Marxism, therefore, is the abolition of these class distinctions and the establishment of a communist society in which full, concrete freedom is realized. Since the proletarian class is seen as the agent of this revolutionary movement, the interests of the proletariat are to be the determining interests in shaping the political and economic life of society so long as classes continue to exist. When the goal of the revolution has been attained the interests of all will be reconciled and conflicts between claims will "wither away." In the interim period of transition to full Communism, however, the special status of the proletariat is to be politically and legally guaranteed. This status is institutionalized by the legal and constitutional "dictatorship of the proletariat." In Marx's words:

> Between capitalist and communist society lies the period of the revolutionary transformation of the one into the other. There corresponds to this also a political transition period in

> which the state can be nothing but *the revolutionary dictatorship of the proletariat.*[40]

As developed by Lenin, the special role of the proletariat in the struggle for socialism is represented by the vanguard of the revolution, the Communist Party. During the period of transition, the Party exercises this leadership by its control of state power. The party assumes the role of

> leading the whole people to socialism, of directing and organizing the new system, of being the teacher, the guide, the leader of all working and exploited people in organizing their social life without the bourgeoisie and against the bourgeoisie.[41]

In Marxist-Leninist thought, therefore, the priority of social participation over political liberty is transformed into a political preeminence of the Communist party.

The Leninist development of Marx's thought was resisted by a number of Marxist thinkers in the early part of this century.[42] It was Lenin, however, and not his critics, who established the basic direction of Soviet Marxism. His conception of the roles of the party and the state as teachers of the way to socialism is still operative in the Soviet Union. It is operative in present day discussions of human rights by representatives of the Soviet Union. For example, Vladimir Kudryavtsev, Director of the Institute of the State and Law of the U.S.S.R. Academy of Sciences, has defined a right as "an opportunity guaranteed by the state to enjoy the social benefits and values existing in a given society." [43] Rights, therefore, are not claims *against* society, whether in the political or economic spheres. They are opportunities to participate in the benefits of the emerging socialist economy and to share in the building of socialism under the direction of state and party.

The first of these opportunities is expressed by the social and economic rights ennumerated in the Soviet constitution. The second opportunity, that of sharing in the building of socialism, sets definite limits to the Soviet conception of civil and political rights.

These limits were succinctly stated by Chairman Brezhnev in his discussion of guarantees of the freedom of expression, press and assembly in the new Soviet constitution:

> Of course, comrades, the draft constitution proceeds from the assumption that the rights and freedoms of citizens cannot and must not be used against our social system or to damage the interests of the Soviet people. That is why the draft says directly, for example, that the exercise of the rights and freedoms by citizens should not damage the interests of society and state and the rights of other citizens, and that political freedoms are granted in accordance with the interests of the people and with the aim of strengthening the socialist system.[44]

Thus in the Soviet Union and other Soviet influenced Marxist nations, political and civil rights are guaranteed to the extent that they are exercised in a way consistent with the building of socialism. This is their positive content. The foundation of this definition is the Marxist analysis of class conflict and the revolutionary effort to create a society truly expressive of the "species nature" of the human person. These rights also possess a negative or defensive content. They are protections of the Soviet people against those who would act contrary to the interests of the developing socialist system.[45] This negative guarantee holds not only against "bourgeois" dissenters but also against government officials who violate socialist law or who use their official positions to cause harm to state or social interests.[46] Soviet leaders and theoreticians, however, continue to regard any wider interpretation of civil and political rights as a class-based ideology designed to protect "the freedom to exploit, the freedom to oppress the people, . . . the freedom of the privileged minority to line its pockets by exploiting the majority." [47]

Like liberal democracy, Soviet theory of human rights is being subjected to internal criticism. The Soviet human rights movement led by such thinkers as Solzhenitsyn, Sakharov, Medvedev, Bukovsky and Amalrik is an unorganized movement. Its participants hold diverse ideological positions, some maintaining their Marxist orthodoxy, others departing from Marxism on various intellectual and religious grounds.[48] There is a common thread which binds them together, however. They are united in their conviction that the identification of state interest with the true interests of society, through the mediation of the party, is a false identification. Such an identification is rooted in the erroneous conviction that the party and the state machinery automatically lead to a just reconciliation of conflicting claims.

Andrei Sakharov has criticized this identification as a perversion of Marx's fundamental principle of the need for full participation by the people in determining the direction of society. In Sakharov's view the need for such participation, and the political and intellectual freedom it presupposes, is even greater in a technological and bureaucratic society than was the case in the days of Marx. As he put it in his well-known essay on *Progress, Coexistence and Intellectual Freedom:*

> Now the diversity and complexity of social phenomena and the dangers facing mankind have become immeasurably greater; and it is therefore all the more important that mankind be protected against the danger of dogmatic and voluntaristic errors, which are inevitable when decisions are reached in a closed circle of secret advisers or shadow cabinets.[49]

Sakharov's rejection of voluntarism harkens back to a fundamental tenet of the mainstream of the Western tradition of human rights. It is the belief that the fundamental values of human existence are not created by the will of any ruler, be it king, parliament, congress or party.

The voluntaristic fallacy against which the Soviet dissidents have raised their voices is the fallacy of confusing fundamental human values with the means by which these values are institutionalized. Government is one of the principal institutional expressions of the social nature of human existence. Legislation, administrative action and judicial decision, whatever form these may take in an individual nation, are indispensable if the interdependence of persons on each other is to have effective institutional expression in society. Marxism's chief contribution to the contemporary human rights debate is its recognition of the need to institutionalize respect for social and economic claims in constitution and law. This important advance on the liberal program has unfortunately led to the confusion of a constitutional order rooted in social interdependence with an absolutist political definition of the nature of social solidarity. Unless the political process by which social policy is defined is a participatory one politics will undercut social interdependence rather than express it.

Marxist thought, of course, denies that genuine social interdependence is possible as long as society and the economy function in accordance with class divisions. If social and economic rights were genuinely guaranteed by the fundamental law of a nation, however, this objection would lose much of its force. Similarly, liberal democracy is built largely on the conviction that a pluralist society cannot easily be brought to agreement on social and economic policies without resorting to totalitarian and tyrannical measures. If, however, protection of the social and economic rights of all were pursued in a way which continued to guarantee basic civil and political liberties, the liberal objections to socialism would be less persuasive. Both of these hypothetical alternatives to the Marxist and Liberal Democratic rights theories rest on the supposition that the recognition of the existence of human rights and the structures of existing economic and political institutions cannot be identified. Both Marxism and liberal democracy prematurely make this identification, though they chose different institutional systems as their point of reference. Liberal democracy notes that not all are willing to have society guarantee social and economic rights and concludes that these rights are not really rights at all. Rights are identified with claims to political liberty. Marxism, on the other hand, notes that unrestricted liberty in a society stratified according to classes leads to a denial of social and economic rights. Political liberty must be restricted if social and economic claims are to be guaranteed. Thus Soviet Marxism has concluded that political and civil rights exist only as grants from the state. In both cases the conclusion is drawn because the institutions of political power are not considered flexible enough to allow the state to guarantee both sets of rights simultaneously.

Thus in both traditions the effective recognition of rights depends on a choice about how political power will be used—in the one case for the protection of claims to individual liberty, in the other for the protection of claims to social participation.

The valid contributions and the limitations of both theories we have been examining suggest that a theory incorporating both perspectives is called for. The urgent need is for a theory of political institutions built on the principle of respect for both sets of claims. As the Soviet dissident Andrei Amalrik has put it in his critique of both the Western democratic and Soviet systems, "everyone who values freedom is confronted by the problem of creating a new ideology which will transcend both liberalism and Communism and make its central issue the indivisible rights of man." [50] The human rights debate, both in the United States and internationally, is in essence a debate about the possibility of creating such a new ideology.

Human Rights and the United Nations

The two traditions we have been examining have been in vigorous interaction at the United Nations during the past thirty years. The United Nations Charter makes promotion of respect for human rights throughout the world one of the fundamental tasks of the community of nations. This goal is set forth in Articles 55 and 56 of the Charter:

> Article 55. With a view to the creation of stability and well-being which are necessary for peaceful and friendly relations among nations based on respect for the principles of equal rights and self-determination of peoples, the United Nations shall promote:
>
> a. higher standards of living, full employment, and conditions of economic and social progress and development;
>
> b. solutions of international economic, social, health, and related problems; and international cultural and educational cooperation; and

c. universal respect for, and observance of, human rights and fundamental freedoms for all without distinction as to race, sex, language, or religion.

Article 56. All members pledge themselves to take joint and separate action in cooperation with the Organization for the achievement of the purpose set forth in Article 55.

It is evident that these goals are far from attained. The divergence in the interpretation given to human rights by the Marxist and liberal democratic traditions has been one of the chief obstacles to the effective pursuit of these goals. The U.N. debates about the foundation and interrelation of rights, however, have revealed both new possibilities and urgent problems in the effort to develop a more adequate theory of human rights.

The tension between these interpretations of rights emerged in the early efforts of the U.N. to spell out the concrete implications of Articles 55 and 56 of the charter. In 1948 the Universal Declaration of Human Rights was approved by the General Assembly as a "common standard of achievement for all peoples and all nations." [51] The foundation of the rights proclaimed in the Universal Declaration is the fact that "All human beings are born free and equal in dignity. They are endowed with reason and conscience and should act towards one another in a spirit of brotherhood" [Article 1]. Articles 3 to 21 go on to list all the rights of the liberal tradition: life, liberty, security of person, property, association, freedom from arbitrary arrest, etc. Articles 22 to 27 add the social and economic rights which are stressed in socialist nations: the rights to social security, work, just wages, education, etc. The Declaration acknowledges, therefore, that a full delineation of human rights must include both negative immunities from coercion and also positive entitlements to participation in the public spheres of the economy, the state and the world of culture. Effective implementation of these social and economic rights depends upon the recognition that "everyone has duties to the community in which alone the free and full development of his personality is possible" [Article 19, 1]. Rights are thus not simply *claims against* other persons, but *claims on* the community as a whole.

The inclusion of both sets of rights in the Declaration was made possible by several political compromises. First, the Declaration was viewed as a manifesto to be used in a program of international education and teaching. It was not to be binding international law subject to enforcement. Enforceable legal obligations were to be spelled out in a separate Covenant. This covenant would bind only those nations which ratified it. Eleanor Roosevelt, chairperson of the commission which drafted the Declaration, described the compromise which led to this two-step effort to create a human rights charter:

> Later it was decided that this Charter should be in two parts, first the Declaration and then the Covenant. The Declaration would set standards and voice aspirations, but would not be legally binding on the nations whose representatives had accepted it in the General Assembly. The Covenant, however, would be drawn in the form of a treaty and would therefore have to be ratified by each nation in whatever way they ratified treaties and it would then be legally binding.[52]

The General Assembly approved the Declaration without a negative vote. Despite the compromise, however, the Soviet Union abstained on the ground that it did not give sufficient emphasis to social-economic rights and remained too much an eighteenth-century document. Seven other nations, including several from Eastern Europe, Saudi Arabia and South Africa, also abstained.[53]

The second compromise between the two traditions was the decision to create not one but two covenants to translate the Declaration into binding law. One was to cover social and economic rights and the other civil and political rights. Both of these covenants were approved by the General Assembly in 1966. They have subsequently been ratified by 44 of the 149 member nations of the U.N. Both have been ratified by the Soviet Union, neither by the United States. Despite these compromises ratification by most nations remains an unfulfilled goal. Many countries, including the United States, have justified their refusal to ratify on the grounds that international supervision of respect for human rights would entail an enfringement of national sovereignty.[54]

Nevertheless, the Universal Declaration has exercised considerable influence in shaping international respect for human rights. A growing number of international lawyers have argued that, though the covenants remain largely unratified, the Universal Declaration has become part of the customary law of nations which is binding on all states. John P. Humphrey, a Canadian jurist who was director of the U.N. Division of Human Rights from 1946 to 1966, has stated the case this way:

> The Declaration and the principles ennunciated in it have been officially invoked on so many occasions both within and outside the United Nations that it can be said that it is the juridical conscience of the international community that the rules ennunciated by it are normatively binding, and this whether they are in fact respected or not. It can be said that the Universal Declaration of Human Rights authentically defines those human rights and fundamental freedoms which the member states of the United Nations undertook to respect and observe by the Charter but which the Charter does not itself define. In retrospect after a quarter of a century, the adoption of the Declaration appears as a much greater achievement than anyone could have imagined in 1948.[55]

Humphrey's American colleague at the Human Rights Division, Egon Schwelb, has argued this position even more vigorously. According to Schwelb's reading of the history of various United Nations agreements on specific human rights issues, the Declaration has been implicitly ratified by the continual references made to it in binding international instruments. In Schwelb's view:

> In the years since 1948 the Universal Declaration has acquired a purpose different from the one which was contemplated and willed by many of the governments that brought it into being in 1948. . . . It can no longer be maintained, whatever the position may have been in 1948, that the Declaration has "only moral force." [56]

Thus both Humphrey and Schwelb argue that a coherent and binding set of norms for the protection of human rights has been gradually evolved at the United Nations. The Universal Declaration, with its inclusive defense of both civil-political and social-economic rights, is on the way to becoming a fundamental standard for the behavior of all nations. President Carter's claim that the human rights violations by nations signatory to the U.N. Charter are not simply internal affairs appears to rest on this kind of analysis.

Nevertheless it is clear that this standard is far from adhered to in many nations of the world. Despite his optimism that revolutionary shifts are taking place in the international law of human rights, Humphrey is compelled to admit that it remains "weak law." [57] This weakness can be traced to a number of causes: the absence of really fundamental and explicit consensus about the content of human rights, the resistance of many countries to all forms of international intervention and limitations on national sovereignty, the lack of truly enforceable legal instruments, the lack of broad-based international concern for human rights, and achievement of a decent standard of living for all with the guaran-twisted by national self-interest.[58] Maurice Cranston has argued that effective implementation of the Universal Declaration is impossible because it contains a fundamental confusion about the relations between rights and legal institutions. In his book, *What Are Human Rights?* Cranston cites all the above mentioned problems which make the international law of human rights weak law. He traces all of them to the inclusion of socio-economic rights in the Declaration.

In Cranston's analysis there is a vast difference between the means needed to guarantee the right to a fair trial or the right of religious liberty and the means which must be called upon to guarantee the right to work or the right to social security. Relatively simple forms of legislation can bring about the protection of civil and political rights, for "since those rights are for the most part rights against government interference with a man's activities, a large part of the legislation needed has to do no more than restrain the government's own executive arm." [59] The protection of social and economic rights, on the other hand, implies that the government "needs to do more than make laws; it has to have access to great capital wealth, and many of the governments of the world today are still poor." [60] Cranston believes that the achievement of a decent standard of living for all with the guarantee of a minimum amount of food, shelter and education is a social ideal of great importance. These ideals, however, are not properly called rights. Thus he argues that the inclusion of social and economic rights in the Declaration has muddied the waters of the human rights debate by calling for something that is presently impossible. This has discredited the very notion of human rights and opened the way for the cynical political use of rights language as mere political rhetoric. In Cranston's words:

> The effect of a Universal Declaration which is overloaded with affirmations of so-called human rights which are not human rights at all is to push *all* talk of human rights out of the clear realm of the morally compelling into the twilight world of utopian aspiration. In the Universal Declaration of 1948 there indeed occurs the phrase "a common standard of achievement" which brands that Delcaration as an attempt to translate rights into ideals. And however else one might choose to define moral rights, they are plainly *not* ideals or aspirations.[61]

For Cranston, the problems encountered in the U.N. human rights debate point out the need to restrict rights claims to those freedoms which have some hope of gaining genuine international protection.

Cranston's argument reveals a crucial issue in the divergence between the liberal democratic and socialist approach to rights. His analysis shows that civil-political rights do not differ from social-economic rights simply on the basis of their content. They also differ in calling for very different modes of political implementation. In the early U.N. debates this difference in modes of implementation was illuminated by distinguishing between "legal rights" and "programme rights." Civil and political rights can be directly translated into law. They are enforceable or justifiable by discrete legislation or judicial decisions. Social and economic rights, however, can only be guaranteed through long range social policies or programs, involving many social and political decisions. Their implementation will necessarily be progressive if it is to happen at all.[62] Liberal democratic thought, with its fundamental principle of the rule of law, has naturally focused on those human rights which can be directly translated into legislation and constitutional principles. Socialist thought, on the other hand, places greater emphasis on the crucial importance of social and economic institutions. It has therefore focused on those rights which demand that these institutions develop in a direction allowing for greater participation by all persons. The U.N. debates point out, therefore, that any adequate theory and program of human rights must recognize that different rights require different means of implementation. Cranston's argument fails to take this into account. "Programme rights" need not be relegated to the "twilight world" of ideals and aspirations simply because they are not realizable by judicial or legislative fiat. This once again points out the importance of not foreshortening the discussion of the theory and foundations of human rights claims by a premature conclusion about how they are to be implemented. This has been made evident at the U.N. precisely in debates about implementation.

The Theoretical Vacuum

The three traditions we have been examining all make major contributions to the development of an adequate theory of human rights. This sketch shows that the three questions with which we began remain central: What is the foundation of human rights? What is the relation between different human rights? What is the relation between human rights and the institutions of social, political and economic life? These questions must be answered if we are to determine which claims are true rights. The United Nations debates have attempted to synthesize the perspectives of both liberal democracy and socialist thought. Though major advances have been made at the U.N. the synthesis remains more of a political compromise than a genuine theoretical breakthrough. It is therefore an unstable synthesis. In the United States, despite presidential and congressional support for both U.N. Covenants, interest in human rights remains largely focused on gross violations of civil and political rights such as *habeas corpus* and freedom of expression. The Soviet Union and other socialist countries continue to justify denial of these rights by appealing to their records in the economic sphere. The situation in some Asian, African and Latin American nations is even more erratic and distressing. The need for a more integral theory of rights which coherently addresses these three questions seems evident. Philosophers and political theorists have a major contribution to make to the development of this more integral and coherent approach. So do various non-governmental organizations active in the work of promoting human rights.

Among these various non-governmental organizations the Roman Catholic Church is notable for the degree to which it has developed an approach to human rights which is both activist and theoretically rigorous. This tradition is far from providing a complete set of answers to all the questions which are present in the current debate. It has, however, sought to take seriously both liberal democratic and socialist perspectives. Because of the Catholic Church's institutional presence throughout the world it has also been compelled to address the question of implementation of rights and "trade off" between rights in a serious way. In hope of adding some further clarification to the current human rights debate we will now turn to an examination of the development of the modern Roman Catholic tradition.

NOTES

1. Ronald Dworkin, *Taking Rights Seriously* (Cambridge, Massachusetts: Harvard University Press, 1977), p. xi.
2. See Joel Feinberg, *Social Philosophy* (Englewood Cliffs, N.J.: Prentice-Hall, 1973), pp. 64-67.
3. "The President's Address to the General Assembly, March 17, 1977," *Weekly Compilations of Presidential Documents* 13 (March 21, 1977), p. 401.
4. *Conference on Security and Cooperation in Europe. Final Act,* 1, (a), VII. Department of State Publication 8826, Aug. 1975, p. 80.
5. Ibid.

6. Universal Declaration of Human Rights, Preamble, in *Human Rights: A Compilation of the International Instruments of the United Nations* (United Nations, New York: United Nations Publications, 1973), Sales No. E. 73. XIV. 2.

7. See Vernon Van Dyke, *Human Rights, the United States and World Community* (New York: Oxford University Press, 1970), pp. 129-141.

8. Iredell Jenkins, "From Natural to Legal to Human Rights," in Erwin H. Pollack, ed. *Human Rights, AMINTAPHIL* 1 (Buffalo, N.Y.: Jay Stewart, 1971), p. 213.

9. Jeremy Bentham, *Anarchical Fallacies,* in Frederick A. Olafson, *Society, Law, and Morality* (Englewood Cliffs, N.J.: Prentice-Hall, 1961), p. 347.

10. *Ibid.,* p. 347.

11. In my analysis of these three approaches I am gratefully indebted to Drew Christiansen, Ronald Garet and Charles Powers. I was fortunate to collaborate with them on the Yale Task Force on Population Ethics. As a group we attempted to analyze the implications of U.N., U.S. Constitutional, Marxist, and Roman Catholic approaches to human rights for population policies. My discussion of liberalism, Marxism and U.N. rights documents has been inspired by the contributions they made to the article published by the Task Force, "Moral Claims, Human Rights and Population Policies" (*Theological Studies* 35, 1974, pp. 83-113). The interpretations presented here depart in a number of ways from their contributions in emphasis but not in substance.

12. There are some commentators who would point out that I am omitting a key political and ideological force that is a (or perhaps the) chief threat to human rights today: the increasing group of States under right wing authoritarian regimes. This kind of regime has been variously described: neo-Fascism, neo-corporatism, the national security state, or, as a Chilean diplomat recently named it, "authoritarian democracy." I agree that a complete analysis should include a discussion of these regimes and their ideologies. For present purposes, however, I think basic issues can be clarified without separate treatment of these regimes.

13. The antecedents of these two documents are complex. They are also different from each other in important ways. For the background from which they emerged see C. B. Macpherson, "Natural Rights in Hobbes and Locke," and John W. Chapman, "Natural Rights and Justice in Liberalism," both in D. D. Raphael, ed., *Political Theory and the Rights of Man* (Bloomington: Indiana Univ. Press, 1967), pp. 1-15 and 27-42. For the roots of the U.S. Constitutional approach to rights in the common law tradition consult Zechariah Chafee, Jr., *How Human Rights Got into the Constitution* (Boston: Boston Univ. Press, 1952), and Ernest Barker, "Natural Law and the American Revolution," in *Traditions of Civility* (Cambridge: Cambridge Univ. Press, 1948), pp. 263-355.

14. John Locke, *Second Treatise on Civil Government,* in Ernest

Barker, ed., *Social Contract: Essays by Locke, Hume and Rousseau* (New York: Oxford Univ. Press, 1962), p. 4.

15. H. L. A. Hart, "Are There Any Natural Rights" in Olafson, *Society, Law and Morality*, p. 173.

16. *Ibid.*, p. 173, note.

17. C. B. Macpherson, "Natural Rights in Hobbes and Locke," p. 5.

18. Isaiah Berlin, "Two Concepts of Liberty," in *Four Essays on Liberty* (New York: Oxford Univ. Press, 1969), p. 125.

19. H. L. A. Hart, "Are There Any Natural Rights?" p. 174, note.

20. John W. Chapman, "Natural Rights and Justice in Liberalism," p. 33.

21. John Rawls, *A Theory of Justice* (Cambridge: The Belknap Press of Harvard Univ. Press, 1971), p. 303.

22. John W. Chapman, "Natural Rights and Justice in Liberalism," p. 42.

23. *Ibid.*, p. 302.

24. *Ibid.*, p. 43.

25. *Ibid.*, p. 302.

26. *Ibid.*, p. 61.

27. Roberto Mangabeira Unger has shown the centrality of this belief in radical pluralism for liberal thought in his *Knowledge and Politics* (New York: Free Press, 1975). It is rooted in what Unger calls "the principle of arbitrary desire," according to which "we cannot determine what to want, or rather we cannot defend our determinations, solely by enlarging our comprehension of facts" (p. 42). See R. M. Hare, *The Language of Morals* (New York: Oxford Univ. Press, 1964), p. 70 and *passim*.

28. Isaiah Berlin, "Two Concepts of Liberty," p. 168.

29. *Ibid.*, p. 171.

30. John Rawls, *A Theory of Justice*, p. 92.

31. *Ibid.*, pp. 152 and 542-43. H. L. A. Hart has carefully examined this tension in Rawls' theory in "Rawls on Liberty and Its Priority," in Norman Daniels, ed. *Reading Rawls: Critical Studies on Rawls' A Theory of Justice* (New York: Basic Books, 1974), pp. 230-252.

32. Rawls is willing to acknowledge that the provisions of a system of equal civil liberties will be of less value to the poor even though these liberties remain real. Norman Daniels has questioned the meaningfulness of this Rawlsian distinction in his "Equal Liberty and Unequal Worth of Liberty," *Reading Rawls*, pp. 253–281.

33. Karl Marx and Friedrich Engels, *The Communist Manifesto*, in Lewis S. Feuer, ed., *Basic Writings on Politics and Philosophy: Karl Marx and Friedrich Engels* (Garden City, N.Y.: Doubleday, Anchor Books, 1959), p. 29.

34. Leonid Brezhnev, "The New Draft Constitution of the U.S.S.R.: The Rights of the State," *Vital Speeches of the Day* XXXXIII (July 1, 1977), p. 548.

35. See Brezhnev, "The New Draft Constitution of the U.S.S.R.," p. 548.

36. See Branko M. Peselj, "Recent Codification of Human Rights in Socialist Constitutions," *Howard Law Journal* 11 (1965), pp. 343–44.

37. Karl Marx, *On the Jewish Question,* in T. B. Bottomore, ed., *Karl Marx: Early Writings* (New York: McGraw-Hill, 1964), p. 25.

38. Karl Marx, *On the Jewish Question,* p. 31.

39. Karl Marx, *Critique of the Gotha Program,* in Feuer, *Basic Writings on Politics and Philosophy,* p. 119.

40. Karl Marx, *Critique of the Gotha Program,* in Feuer, *Basic Writings on Politics and Philosophy,* p. 127.

41. V. I. Lenin, *The State and Revolution* in *Selected Works,* One Volume Edition (New York: International Publishers, 1971), p. 281.

42. For an account of these debates see George Lichtheim, *Marxism: An Historical and Critical Study,* second edition, (New York: Praeger, 1965), chap. 8.

43. Vladimir Kudryavtsev, "The Truth About Human Rights," *Human Rights* 5 (1976), p. 199.

44. Leonid Brezhnev, "The New Draft Constitution of the U.S.S.R.," p. 548.

45. See Branko M. Peselj, "Recent Codification of Human Rights in Socialist Constitutions," p. 345.

46. See Harold Berman, "Human Rights in the Soviet Union," *Howard Law Journal* 11 (1965), pp. 333-341.

47. R. Kulikov, "Man's Inalienable Rights," *International Affairs,* April 1977, p. 32.

48. For an informative study of this movement see Valery Chalidze, *To Defend These Rights: Human Rights and the Soviet Union,* trans. Guy Daniels (New York: Random House, 1974).

49. Andrei Sakharov, *Progress, Coexistence and Intellectual Freedom,* trans. by The New York Times (New York: W. W. Norton, 1968), pp. 61-62.

50. Andrei Amalrik, "By Bread Alone? A Well-Fed Slave Is a Well-Fed Slave," *New York Times,* Feb. 3, 1977, p. 33. This article is an abbreviated version of Mr. Amalrik's speech on accepting the 1976 Human Rights Award of the International League for Human Rights.

51. "Universal Declaration of Human Rights," Preamble, in *Human Rights: A Compilation of International Instruments of the United Nations,* p. 1.

52. Eleanor Roosevelt, "Human Rights," in Robert E. Sherwood, ed., *Peace on Earth* (New York: Heritage House, 1949), pp. 65-66.

53. See Eleanor Roosevelt, "Human Rights," p. 67.

54. For a discussion of the history of resistance to ratification in the United States see Vernon Van Dyke, *Human Rights, the United States, and World Community,* chap. 7.

55. John P. Humphrey, "The Revolution in the International Law of Human Rights," *Human Rights* 4 (1975), pp. 207-208.

56. Egon Schwelb, *Human Rights and the International Community: The Roots and Growth of the Universal Declaration of Human Rights, 1948-1963* (Chicago: Quadrangle Books, 1964), pp. 37 and 47.

57. Humphrey, "The Revolution in the International Law of Human Rights," p. 210.

58. For a discussion of these points see Louis Henkin, "The United States and the Crisis in Human Rights," *Virginia Journal of International Law* 14 (1974), pp. 653-671.

59. Maurice Cranston, *What Are Human Rights?* (New York: Taplinger Publishing Co., 1973), p. 66.

60. Cranston, *What Are Human Rights?,* pp. 66-67.

61. Cranston, *What Are Human Rights?,* p. 68.

62. For a helpful discussion of this distinction see J. E. S. Fawcett, "The International Protection of Human Rights," in D. D. Raphael, *Political Theory and the Rights of Man,* pp. 127-129.

Part Two
Retrieval

Chapter Two
The Development of the Roman Catholic Rights Theory

In the Spring of 1963 Pope John XXIII issued the encyclical letter *Pacem in Terris*. Addressing all Catholics, Christians and "men of good will" throughout the world, Pope John set forward the most powerful and thorough statement of the Roman Catholic understanding of human rights in modern times. *Pacem in Terris* boldly affirms a wide variety of rights, including the right to life, the rights to food, clothing, shelter, rest and medical care, the rights to culture and education, the rights to freedom of expression, association and the free exercise of religion, the right to work, organize and form labor unions, the right to private property and the right to juridical protection of all one's human rights. The reception given John XXIII's human rights charter was remarkable. The response was so positive not only because the encyclical cut across the ideological battle lines of our time but also because it did so with intellectual rigor and persuasive power. The non-Christian political philosopher Maurice Cranston, though not fully in agreement with all that the Pope had to say about social and economic rights, described it as "a work of intellectual force to compare with *Zum Ewige Friede* of Immanuel Kant, and of topical significance and urgency unrivaled by the speeches of any living statesman."[1]

Pacem in Terris did not spring full-grown from the heads of Pope John and his theological advisors. The understanding of human rights it contains has roots all the way back to Thomas Aquinas, Augustine, the Bible and Aristotle. More proximately, it emerged from the social doctrine of the modern papacy. The writings of popes from Leo XIII to John XXIII himself were the chief sources from which *Pacem in Terris* drew for its understanding of human rights. Since 1963 the Catholic rights tradition has continued to develop. The Second Vatican Council, the writings of Pope Paul VI and the deliberations of the international Synod of Bishops have subsequently given the tradition a deeper theological foundation and a more adequate awareness of the importance of conflict and power in social life.

This chapter will trace the development of the Roman Catholic rights theory over the past one hundred years. The focus will be on the official teachings of the Church as expressed in papal, conciliar and synodal documents. The teachings, of course, were put forward in response to significant social and political events. This social context shaped both the content and the tone of the teachings. The documents cannot be adequately understood without attending to this context. The concern here, however, is principally with the intellectual history of the Catholic theory of rights. Analysis of the social events and movements which conditioned the theoretical formulations of the tradition will therefore be subordinate to the task of identifying the ethical concepts and arguments presented by the documents. In the third chapter the theological underpinnings of the ethical arguments will be explored.

The thread that ties all these documents together is their common concern for the protection of the dignity of the human person. In a speech delivered in May 1961, John XXIII stated that the entire modern tradition "is always dominated by one basic theme—an unshakable affirmation and vigorous defense of the dignity and rights of the human person." [2] In John XXIII's view, human dignity is the concrete normative value which the entire tradition has attempted to defend. Respect for the dignity and worth of the person is the foundation of all the specific human rights and more general social ethical frameworks adopted by the encyclicals and other Church teachings. These rights and ethical frameworks have undergone a notable evolution and will continue to do so. But through this process all alterations have been governed by an attempt to remain responsive to human dignity and its concrete demands. Pope John's encyclical *Mater et Magistra* identifies the thread of continuity clearly:

> The cardinal point of this teaching is that individual men are necessarily the foundation, cause and end of all social institutions. We are referring to human beings, insofar as they are social by nature, and raised to an order of existence which transcends and subdues nature. Beginning with this very basic principle whereby the dignity of the human person is affirmed and defended, Holy Church, especially during the last century . . . has arrived at clear social teachings whereby the mutual relationships of men are ordered.[3]

The concern of this chapter will be to discover how the foundational value of human dignity was interpreted at different stages in the tradition's development. It will also study why particular claims came to be regarded as indispensable for the protection of this dignity and therefore as human rights.

LEO XIII: THE PRIMACY OF THE PERSONAL

The history of modern Roman Catholic teaching about human rights begins with the pontificate of Leo XIII (1878—1903). It was with Leo XIII that the Church began to move from a stance of adamant resistance to modern Western developments in political and social life to a stance of critical participation in them. This movement had two flanks. The first faced toward the rising aspirations for political equality represented by the liberal democratic movements which began with the French Revolution. The second looked toward the movements for economic equality and socialism stimulated by the growing industrialization of society during the nineteenth century. These two movements occasioned significant developments in Catholic thought about the political and economic rights of all persons.

Leo's positive affirmations about the political implications of human dignity are summarized in a phrase from the 1891 encyclical *Rerum Novarum* which has been cited many times in the later documents of the tradition: "Man precedes the State." [4] The worth of human beings, in other words, is the standard by which political and legal institutions are to be evaluated. Politics and law are to serve persons. Persons do not exist to serve the political and legal order. The human person is never simply of functional or utilitarian value. Human beings possess a transcendental worth not hypothetically subordinate to any other end. This affirmation of transcendental personal worth is most clearly evident in Leo's condemnation of various social and political arrangements in which persons are made instrumental. Perhaps the most notable of these themes in his writings is the opposition to all subordination of the person to an absolutist state. In his careful analysis of Leo XIII's social writings, John Courtney Murray has characterized this central concern of the Leonine corpus as resistance to "totalitarian democracy." [5] It is also evident in Leo's interpretation of the forms of socialism prevalent in his time.

Leo's association of democracy with absolutism was occasioned by particular forms of democratic thought prevalent in his day—especially that of Bakunin, who was active in organizing anarchist groups in Italy at this time.[6] Anticlericalism and opposition to any public role for the Church was also a common aspect of democratic movements stemming from the French Revolution.[7] Thus Leo XIII's criticisms were inspired in large part by his desire to protect the Church's freedom to pursue its religious mission and by the political self-interest of the papacy. In its theoretical elaboration, however, Leo's critique was directed against all forms of democratic theory which maintain that basic values and human rights are created by human choice. It was an objection to all forms of strict moral and political voluntarism. As Leo saw it, once the voluntarist supremacy of human choice and liberty is made the exclusive foundation of political life there can be no defense of the person against the supremacy of the will of those who have the greater numbers. Unless the dignity of the person is a wider and more inclusive reality than normless human liberty, "the law determining what is right to do and avoid doing is at the mercy of the majority. Now this is simply a road leading straight to tyranny." [8] Such subordination is an attack on the very foundation of social and political life as it is conceived in the papal tradition. Only when legal and political structures are in service of *all* persons are they properly ordered. Social organizations must be responsive to the moral claim of human dignity as a noninstrumental value. Otherwise they will become both totalitarian and oppressive. Thus human persons "precede" the state by virtue of the primacy of the moral claim of every person to respect for his or her transcendental worth.

Leo's understanding of the implications of this foundational primacy of the person, however, contained an unresolved tension. This tension was centered in his understanding of equality. On the one hand, he affirmed the equal dignity of all persons. This is especially true in *Rerum Novarum,* where he stated that all have an equal claim to the products of their labor: "In this respect all men are equal; there is no difference between rich and poor, master and servant, ruled and ruler." [9] In addition, all persons stand equal before the law: "As regards the State, the interests of all, whether high or low, are equal. The members of the working classes are citizens by nature and by the same right as the rich." [10] At the same time, Leo XIII associated the egalitarian claims of the democratic movements with the most libertarian of the descendants of the French Revolution. He thought that in identifying equality of dignity with the primacy of liberty these groups were undermining the moral foundations of government. Thus Leo XIII continued to defend the legitimacy of unequal political rights, for he could not conceive of a form of egalitarian democracy which did not subordinate the dignity of minorities to the will of the majority.[11]

Leo's view of the concrete implications of equal human dignity, therefore, was structured through his understanding of the means available for institutionalizing social relationships. A hierarchical understanding of social order provided the only framework within which he believed human dignity could be defended. In the economic sphere and before the law, equality received major emphasis. In Leo's treatment of social order, class, and the distribution of the benefits of higher culture, the paternalistic or hierarchical emphasis prevailed. This second aspect of his thought was asserted against forces attempting to reduce or eliminate the privileged role of the Church in European society. John Courtney Murray has analyzed this tension and concluded that it led to two different concepts of the role of government in Leo's writings.[12] The ambiguity of Leo's understanding of equality was not fully resolved in the Catholic tradition until the middle of the twentieth century in the writings of Pius XII. But Leo XIII's fundamental moral norm of human dignity was a genuine source of the development of the social interpretation which brought this resolution about.

It was on the economic flank of the Church's engagement with modern society, therefore, that Leo made the most substantive advances. The positive influence toward equality exerted by his writings came chiefly from his treatment of the economic and social rights of workers. Human dignity gives persons a claim to be protected by the state against those who would reduce them to instruments for their own purposes. "No man may with impunity outrage that dignity which God Himself treats with great reverence."[13] Leo XIII developed this aspect of his thought chiefly in *Rerum Novarum*. In this encyclical a line of thought was begun which culminated in John XXIII's comprehensive treatment of socioeconomic rights.

For several decades prior to the date when *Rerum Novarum* was issued, groups of "social Catholics" had been formulating an approach to the new economic realities of industrial capitalism which sought to ameliorate the frequently appalling conditions of the lives of workers.[14] A central goal of the social Catholic movement was to shape a moral theory which would unite the claims of human dignity with a social theory adequate to the new industrial situation.[15] Through the lenses provided by the research and discussion of these groups Leo XIII was led to see that a radical failure to respect the claims of personal dignity was present in the economic organization of the Europe of his time. Solutions would be difficult to come by, but the problem was painfully evident:

> In any case we clearly see, and on this there is general agreement, that some opportune remedy must be found for the misery and wretchedness pressing so unjustly on the majority of the working-class. . . . By degrees it has come to pass that workingmen have been surrendered, isolated and helpless, to the hardheartedness of employers and the greed of unchecked competition. The mischief has been increased

> by rapacious usury, which, although more than once condemned by the Church, is nevertheless, under a different guise, but with like unjustice, still practiced by covetous and grasping men. To this must be added that the hiring of labor and the conduct of trade are concentrated in the hands of comparatively few; so that a small number of very rich men have been able to lay upon the teeming masses of poor [*infinitae proletariorum multitudini*] a yoke little better than slavery itself.[16]

The offensiveness of this situation is clearly the "wretchedness and misery" to which the workers are being subjected. But at a more fundamental level this suffering is itself objectionable because persons have a justified claim on others not to be reduced to such a condition. Leo's comparison of the situation to one of slavery brings out the foundation of his moral objection. Persons have a transcendental worth which entitles them not to be treated simply as means to the economic well-being of others. The outrage of the situation is that this fundamental dignity is being violated. Leo put his position more positively in another paragraph of *Rerum Novarum:* "The first thing of all to secure is to save unfortunate working people from the cruelty of men of greed, who use human beings as mere instruments for money making." [17]

The result of this attempt to relate the fundamental moral norm of human dignity to the concrete conditions of the time was the formulation of a number of quite specific rights and duties in the economic sphere. In this formulation two distinct factors were brought together: the norm of human dignity and a theory of social interaction and social institutions. The task of the encyclical was to clarify "the relative rights and mutual duties of the rich and of the poor, of capital and labor." [18] These rights and duties were seen as the demands of human dignity refracted and differentiated through the concrete structures of human existence in nature, society and the economic sphere.

Among the rights defended in *Rerum Novarum* were the right to adequate remuneration for one's labor and the right to retain the results of labor in the form of private property. Furthermore, the encyclical calls for the extension of actual property ownership to as great a number of persons as possible. The right to private property derives not simply from the freedom of individual persons to act in a way unimpeded by others, but also from the fact that persons necessarily depend for the preservation of their dignity upon material conditions. All have a right to have these needs fulfilled at least minimally. Thus the encyclical affirms the existence of rights to adequate food, clothing, and shelter.[19] These rights are derived from an analysis of necessary relationships between human dignity and its conditions and limits. Such relationships mean that the moral standard for the evaluation of the adequacy of wages is not simply freedom of contractual agreement. The preservation of human dignity demands that contracts recognize these necessary material conditions. This is the foundation of *Rerum Novarum*'s argument for the right to a just wage:

> Let the working man and the employer make free agreements, and in particular let them agree freely as to the wages; nevertheless, there underlies a dictate of natural justice more imperious and ancient than any bargain between man and man, namely that wages ought not to be insufficient to support a frugal and well-behaved wage earner.[20]

Without the recognition of this right, the freedom to enter into wage contracts will become empty of practical significance for a large number of poor and powerless persons. Thus the critique of voluntarism which Leo XIII directed against political absolutism is also at the foundation of his theory of social and economic rights.

To each of these rights corresponds a duty. Employers are under an obligation to recognize and protect each of these rights. The encyclical, however, is not content with leaving the recognition of these rights to the good will of employers. Workers have the further right to organize associations or unions to defend their just claims. This is a specific form of the more general right of association which belongs to all human persons as both self-determining and social beings.[21] Also, the state may and should legitimately intervene to protect the common good, which consists in the mutual respect of rights and the fulfillment of duties by all citizens.[22] The state, moreover, has a special obligation to defend the rights of the poor and the powerless:

> Rights must be religiously respected wherever they exist, and it is the duty of public authority to prevent and to punish injury, and to protect everyone in the possession of his own. Still, when there is question of defending the rights of individuals, the poor have a claim to especial consideration. The richer classes have many ways of shielding themselves, and stand less in need of help from the State; whereas the mass of the poor have no resources of their own to fall back upon, and must chiefly depend upon the assistance of the State. And it is for this reason that wage earners, since they mostly belong to the class of the needy, should be specially cared for and protected by the government.[23]

This principle of preferential protection of the poor shows once again that the negative conception of liberty characteristic of liberal thought is not the only criterion of either human rights or governmental interventions in the writings of Leo XIII. In effect, Leo XIII anticipated the Rawlsian argument for the priority of liberty over social and economic rights and rejected it.

In summary, Leo's encyclicals laid the groundwork for the modern Catholic theory of human rights. Human dignity is the foundation of this theory. The defense of dignity was the source of his objections to the liberal theory of the state and its overriding concern with the preservation of liberty negatively understood. It was also the foundation of his strong affirmations of the basic economic rights to food, clothing, shelter, organization, and a living wage. In both the political and the economic spheres the demands of human dignity were interpreted with the help of an analysis of the impact of social, economic and political institutions on human persons. This interpretation led to very notable advances in Church thought in the economic sphere. In the political and cultural spheres, however, his writings continue the classical association of Catholic thought with a hierarchical and traditionalist model of social organization.

Leo XIII's two successors, Pius X (1903–1914) and Benedict XV (1914–1922), made few notable advances in the Catholic rights theory. Pius X's social writings can be characterized as an attempt to bring about a "*restauration*" of more traditional theoretical frameworks and theological interpretations of the basis of Christian morality.[24] It is clear that Pius X solved the problem of the tension between the egalitarian and hierarchical conceptions of society present in Leo XIII's writings by opting firmly for hierarchy and traditionalism.[25] Benedict XV devoted the social efforts of his pontificate to the formulation of a series of peace proposals which attempted to aid in the reconciliation of the conflict of World War I. It was not until Pius XI came on the scene that the development began by Leo XIII resumed.

PIUS XI: SOCIAL JUSTICE

The years during which Pius XI was pope (1922–1939) were dominated by three new social developments of massive significance—the great depression, the consolidation of the Russian Revolution into a successful communist regime, and the emergence of Fascist dictatorships in Italy and Germany. Each of these developments had a complex series of causes. Each was accompanied by political consequences of tragic and extensive proportions. The Roman Catholic understanding of human rights developed rapidly during this period under the pressure of these events.[26] In the midst of the various attempts to respond to his many-sided historical situation, Pius XI continued to give major emphasis to the centrality of human dignity as the basis of all human rights.

Pius XI's most influential encyclical, *Quadragesimo Anno* (1931), focused on the economic patterns which lay behind the worldwide depression and by which the dignity of the person was oppressed and threatened. This encyclical oscillated between optimism over the progress which had been made in the area of labor relations during the time since *Rerum Novarum* and pessimism based upon the experience of the depths of the great depression. The pervasive violations of personal dignity were the result, in Pius XI's analysis, of patterns of domination of one group of persons by another. These patterns thrust large numbers of persons into a state of "hand-to-mouth uncertainty which is the lot of the proletarian." [27] They were in fact an instrumentalizing of some persons to ends set by others. It was the structure of the economy which lay behind this result which drew forth some of Pius XI's strongest words:

> It is patent that in our days not alone is wealth accumulated, but immense power and despotic economic domination are concentrated in the hands of a few, and that these few are frequently not the owners, but only the trustees and directors of invested funds, which they administer at their good pleasure. This domination becomes particularly irresistible when exercised by those who, because they hold the control money, are able to govern credit and determine its allotment, for that reason supplying, so to speak, the life blood of the entire economic body, and grasping, as it were, in their hands, the very soul of production, so that no one dare breathe against their will.[28]

These patterns of domination in the economic sphere are morally objectionable because they functionalize human persons. They are not *simply* a denial of the legitimate needs which persons have for material well-being of a certain minimum level or for the economic stability which is a psychological necessity of humane existence. The patterns of domination and proletarianization do indeed have these consequences. In and through these functional or consequentialist criteria, however, Pius XI is pointing to a more fundamental objection to this sort of economic situation: it violates personhood as such. All of Pius XI's claims about respect for persons' claims to material, bodily and even psychological necessities are ultimately founded on a characteristic of the person which transcends any and all of these needs. Persons have needs which must be respected. But these needs must be respected because human beings in their radically personal constitution are more than a collection of needs.[29] They are spiritual or transcendental as well as material beings, and must never be totally subordinated to the functional desires or needs of other persons.

The defense of the transcendental worth of the person thus led Pius XI to a vigorous critique of theories of moral obligation and social organization associated with liberal, competitive capitalism. But these theories were not the only targets of the Pope's critique. In his view, Marxism and socialism in their various forms had also wandered from the path of respect for human dignity.[30] There are obvious parallels between aspects of Marxist thought and Pius XI's views on the conditions of the proletariat and the destructiveness of unbridled competition. But like Leo XIII, Pius XI rejected the theory of class struggle adopted by Marxism-Leninism. This was undoubtedly the result of the close links between the Church and the classes which were the targets of the Marxist attack. These links prevented the papal tradition from understanding important aspects of Marxist social analysis. In addition to these social causes of the rejection of class warfare, the theory was rejected on moral grounds as a denial in principle of the dignity of the persons of an entire class. The pope did not explicitly consider the issue in terms of strategy or usefulness in explaining patterns of social change, but rather in terms of its implications for the understanding of the nature of moral obligation. In its most radical form the theory of class struggle and the dictatorship of the proletariat is a denial of the relevance of the dignity of the persons of one social group to the strategies of another.[31]

As Pius XI read the socialists, their politics were linked with a materialistic concept of the person. Consequently, in order to defend transcendental personal worth he felt compelled to reject all forms of socialism including the more moderate revisionist versions.[32] He believed that even in these varieties, socialism overruns human dignity. The Pope's understanding of what revisionist socialism proposed can be challenged, but his positive affirmation is clear.[33] It was a defense of the fundamental norm that neither in production nor in social relationships nor in political life may the person be subordinated to nonpersonal ends. It is also clear that Pius XI did not intend to defend an individualistic notion of the person. Social life is constitutive of the dignity of the human person, for persons are always and everywhere social. Social and political organization must be subordinated to the good of the persons who compose society, not the other way around. This positive affirmation

> must not be understood in the sense of liberalistic individualism, which subordinates society to the selfish use of the individual; but only in the sense that by means of an organic union with society and by mutual collaboration, the attainment of earthly happiness is placed within the reach of all.[34]

It is "only man, the human person"[35] who is an adequate moral measure of all forms of social organization and interrelation. As Pius XI understood them, socialist and communist views violate this fundamental principle as thoroughly as do the theories of liberal politics and economics. In so doing they "rob human personality of all its dignity" and reduce the person to "a mere cogwheel" in the social system.[36]

The centrality of the dignity of the person also shaped Pius XI's approach to the development of the Fascist and Nazi dictatorships. His relationships with both Mussolini and Hitler have been the subject of heated controversy. Our concern here is not to adjudicate between the various claims which have been made about these relationships nor to judge the adequacy of the arguments about the historical questions which are quite legitimately presented at a high emotional pitch.[37] Pius XI was specially concerned to assure the freedom of the Catholic Church in his arguments with these regimes and thus was too ready to compromise when he succeeded in obtaining concessions for the Church. Nonetheless, the Leonine theme of opposition to all forms of state absolutism was reasserted and even intensified in opposition to the Fascist dictatorships. *Non Abbiamo Bisogno* (1931) was directed to the situation prevailing in the early days of Fascist rule in Italy. Here Pius XI accessed the Fascist government of following a policy based on "statolatry" in its demands that all education be under state supervision.[38] A similar critique of the glorification of the state in Nazi Germany was developed in *Mit Brennender Sorge* (1937):

> Whoever exalts race, or the people, or the state, or a particular form of the state, or the depositories of power, or any other fundamental value of the human community—however necessary and honorable be their function in worldly things—whoever raises these notions above their standard values and divinizes them to an idolatrous level, distorts and perverts an order of the world planned and created by God: he is far from the true faith in God and from the concept of life which that faith upholds.[39]

Here Nazism is being attacked because of its absolutization of functional or relative values and its subordination of the worth of the person to these divinized reifications. State, race, and structures of power are not evil in themselves. They become evil when they fail to serve their moral purpose: the protection and enhancement of human dignity.

The critique of the economic causes of the depression, of Marxism and of Fascism, however, was not limited to negative responses of this sort nor to the reassertion of the fundamental norm of human dignity in Pius XI's writings. His writings, like Leo XIII's, contain a number of quite concrete and positive specifications of the moral claims of human dignity. The most significant change in the discussion of the positive demands of human dignity in the encyclicals of Pius XI was the result of his development of the notion of "social justice" into a key ethical concept in Catholic social thought.[40] In Catholic ethics this term has come to have a more technical meaning than it does in general contemporary discussions. The concept of social justice is a conceptual tool by which moral reasoning takes into account the fact that relationships between persons have an institutional or structural dimension. Efforts to specify the content of human rights must occur within the context of these institutional dynamics. For example, the determination of specific rights and duties in the economic sphere cannot be made without including an analysis of the dynamics of the economy as a whole. Pius XI's use of the notion of social justice, therefore, indicates the emergence of a new sensitivity in Catholic thought to the possibility of conscious institutional change. It was the beginning of an important departure from Leo XIII's frequent appeal to traditionalist justifications for a hierarchical social order.

For example, in Pius XI's understanding, the right to private ownership of property will necessarily have different implications in a premonetized economy, in a feudal system and in an industrial society.[41] In all of these situations it is necessary to recognize that the moral purpose of ownership is twofold: it is a form of protection for personal self-determination and it is a means by which society is organized to fulfill basic human needs.[42] Thus the extent of the right of private ownership must be determined with reference both to personal freedom *and* social strategies for fulfilling basic human needs. Social justice demands that the economy be directed and structured in such a way that both of these purposes are attained. The state has the ultimate responsibility for assuring that these demands are met.[43]

The notion of social justice as a regulative principle for societal institutions is based on the conviction that human dignity is a social rather than a purely private affair. Human dignity makes a genuine moral demand upon the organizational patterns by which public life is structured. This moral demand must be responded to through a social effort coordinated by government. The concept of social justice thus points to the fact that human rights have a social as well as individual foundation. It also indicates that the protection of human rights will be possible only through a process of social development and that government has a properly moral role to play in bringing about such a process.

Thus it is evident that Pius XI was struggling with the major issues in the human rights debate outlined in Chapter One. In his opposition to the various forms of totalitarianism he reaffirmed Leo XIII's stress on the primacy of human dignity. At the same time, his use of the concept of social justice marks a major advance in the tradition's understanding of the way social institutions mediate the claims of human dignity and shape the content of human rights. In *Quadragesimo Anno* Pius XI reaffirmed the rights stated in *Rerum Novarum,* but with a new sensitivity to their social conditions and limits. In *Divini Redemptoris* he provided a list of rights which, though incomplete and unsystematic, reveals the continuity with Leo XIII: the right to life, to bodily integrity, to the necessary means of existence; the right to tend toward one's ultimate goal in the path marked out by God; the right of association and the right to possess and use property.[44] These rights can be realized only in society. They make demands on the kinds of social order which should exist and are limited by the fact of their social interrelation. This general perspective was especially operative in Pius XI's arguments concerning the right to a just wage, the right to organize and the economic role of government. We shall point out in Chapter Four, there are still notable elements of a hierarchical conception of the way conflict between rights should be reconciled. But Pius XI's writings represent a major development in the tradition's recognition of the social conditions and limits which enter into the specification of the meaning of human dignity and human rights.

PIUS XII: A COMMUNITY OF MORALLY RESPONSIBLE CITIZENS

The central theme of respect for the dignity of the person as the foundation of all moral order was taken up and vigorously affirmed by the next pope, Pius XII. During his pontificate (1939–1958) Pius XII spoke more frequently and more systematically of the moral roots of social, political and economic order than had any of his predecessors. In Pius XII's writings and speeches the dignity of the person was lifted from the level of a basic but frequently implicit first principle of Roman Catholic social morality to the level of explicit and formal concern.[45] His writings and speeches were a response to both the horrors of the World War and to the increasingly repressive character of the Stalinist regime in the Soviet Union. His discussions of human rights were also a response to the precarious situation of the Church in Eastern Europe after the war. These conditions set the stage for a much deeper appropriation and explicitation of the importance of constitutional government than had been present in earlier writings of the modern papacy.

Pius XII's approach to social morality was most characteristically revealed in his Christmas Address of 1942.[46] At a time when the conflict of World War II was heading toward its savage climax, the Pope turned to an examination of the basic principles of the internal order of nations which he saw as prerequisites for lasting international peace. This order must grow out of a recognition of the dignity of all persons within society. It cannot be imposed mechanically or by force. Such a superimposed order is "fictitious"—in reality it would be a form of disorder.[47] Thus Pius XII put forward a conception of social and juridical order which is dynamic and living. It is far removed from that of political theories which view order primarily as a "restrainer" of evil or as essentially coercive. These functions of order are legitimate in the Pope's view but only to the extent that they remain rooted in and consistent with full respect for the dignity of persons. Without such respect, order will inevitably create the conditions of its own demise.[48]

Pius XII developed this view in his treatment of the moral basis of the juridical or legal structures which are necessary to guarantee and support social harmony. The role of law is to support and strengthen forms of social interrelation which are based on a mutual recognition and respect for the dignity of the human person.[49] Such a view entails a rejection of the views of legal positivism in which the legitimacy of law is based on its simple existence as law rather than on a pre-legal moral criterion. His view of the state, however, was not moralistic. His rejection of legal positivism was accompanied by a simultaneous and correlative rejection of moral subjectivism. The criterion of morality is the human person, not a private understanding of morality derived from sectarian principles which would then be imposed on society by coercive means. Following Leo XIII and Pius XI, Pius XII's understanding of social morality is essentially public. Also like his two predecessors, he was firmly opposed to all sectarianism, whether in its religious or secular forms.[50] This understanding of law is of a piece with his rejection of positivistic accounts of the nature of moral obligation, again whether such accounts be legal, philosophical or religious.

It was one of Pius XII's great fears that such a person-centered public morality was gravely threatened by the patterns of social organization of his contemporary world. In his view, the power of modern technology was contributing to the development of this threat in a way not present in previous periods. In social and economic life the subordination of the person to the requirements of the logic of technological growth was frequently decried by the Pope, especially in his later writings. The technological spirit has the social consequence of creating a new form of social existence: that of mass or anonymous man. As early as his first encyclical, *Summi Pontificatus,* issued in 1939, Pius XII was speaking darkly of his age as one of "spiritual emptiness and deep-felt interior poverty." [51] This sense of lostness was seen as the result of a social and political situation which had uprooted persons from a living sense of their mutual dignity and reduced society to something purely "physical and mechanical." [52] Persons were more and more reduced to being "mere cogs in the various social organizations."[53]

This negative view of technological change and the frequent condemnation of the totalitarian or absolutist state were the dominant objections made by Pius XII to modern social developments. His view was shared by a number of European philosophers of the same period, both Christian and non-Christian.[54] Pius XII, however, struck a considerably more constructive note than some of these technological critics. His critique had a positive content and he proposed both a social and a juridical alternative to the negative elements he rejected.

This positive alternative was based on a vision of life in society as that of a "community of morally responsible citizens." [55] Pius XII's statements on the foundation of familial, economic and legal structures in the responsible respect for persons was proposed as a way beyond the threat of depersonalization and mechanization. Though often negative in tone, Pius XII strongly affirmed the possibility of embodying respect for persons in the various levels of social organizations. This positive aspect of his thought brought out an essential characteristic of the moral theory of the modern papacy. Respect for the dignity of the person is not to be thought of as an ideal to be approximated or approached asymptotically by the patterns of social organization. It is rather an intrinsic element in the very nature of organization itself.[56] All forms of social life are conceived of as essentially moral relationships. They are in service of the dignity of human persons whenever they conform to their own proper inner structure.

Such an approach to social morality is unworkable outside the context of a "community of morally responsible citizens." Clearly, Pius XII's hopes for the possibility of realizing such a community would have been "dreaming innocence" [57] were it not for the fact that he saw the establishment of such a community as a task of developing forms of organization which both condition and limit human freedom. His vision of a society in which human dignity is respected was neither an anarchist paradise nor the Marxist eschaton which will arrive after the withering away of the state. The task of respecting human dignity is a moral task present *within* the conditions and limits of human life. Thus the achievement of the goal is not an impossible ideal, but a realizable moral imperative. The conditions and limits of the human situation are built into the concept of morality which is operative here. Respect for human dignity occurs within and through these conditions and limits. Though human dignity is of transcendental worth it remains a *finite* good. A community in which such respect is embodied is not one in which human finititude is overthrown. Though the moral claim that this dignity makes for respect is unconditional, it is a claim which is structured and conditioned by the limitations and possibilities of persons in society.[58] It is structured by that finite form of mutuality which is transcendental dignity's human form.

These finite conditions which are necessary for the promotion of human dignity are human rights. Pius XII did not give a systematic treatment of all such rights in his statements. He did, however, devote considerable effort to clarifying the fundamental forms of human interrelationship which organize and internally condition human dignity. The social institutions of family, property, association and government were seen by him as permanent elements through which the moral community of responsible persons is ordered.[59] An analysis of the ways in which these institutions influence the core value of human dignity led to the specification of a number of human rights and corresponding duties in his writings.

For example, in his Christmas address of 1942, Pius XII stated that respect for the dignity of persons entails

> respect for and the practical realization of the following fundamental personal rights: the right to maintain and develop one's corporal, intellectual and moral life and especially the right to religious formation and education; the right to worship God in private and public and to carry on religious works of charity; the right to marry and to achieve the aim of married life; the right to conjugal and domestic society; the right to work, as the indispensable means toward the maintainance of family life; the right to free choice of a state of life, and hence, too, of the priesthood or religious life; the right to the use of material goods, in keeping with his duties and social limitations.[60]

The same address also affirmed that each person has a right to a governmental or juridical system which protects all of these personal rights from attack. The various dimensions of such a juridical order were specified in a later address:

> The right to existence, the right to one's good name, the right to one's own culture and national character, the right to develop oneself, the right to demand observance of international treaties, and other like rights, are demanded by the law of nations, dictated by nature itself.[61]

The order, then, which Pius XII saw as the concrete realization of social morality is a juridical or constitutional order of rights. The realization of such an order is a duty incumbent on all persons, and this duty is to be carried out in a partial but very important way through constitutional government.

The activity of the state is both based on and limited by these fundamental human rights. It is this view which enabled Pius XII to understand government as a moral activity rather than as a mechanical scale on which various competing interests are weighed. The role of government is the promotion of the common good—that form of society in which responsible citizens act in a way which leads to mutual respect for rights and dignity. The common good, since it is founded on mutual dignity, is not in opposition to human rights, but rather their guarantee.

> To safeguard the inviolable sphere of the rights of the human person and to facilitate the fulfillment of his duties should be the essential office of public authority. Does this not follow from the genuine concept of the common good which the State is called upon to promote? Hence it follows that the care of such a common good does not imply a power so extensive over the members of the community that in virtue of it the public authority can interfere with the evolution of individual activity such as we have just described. . . . To deduce such extension of power from the care of the common good would be equivalent to overthrowing the very meaning of the word.[62]

This self-limiting concept of the common good and the role of government in protecting it shows that, for Pius XII as well as for the entire tradition, human rights cannot be understood apart from social interdependence, nor can social well-being be understood apart from personal rights. The obvious difficulty with this position is that, *as a principle,* it does not *specify* how conflicts between individual and social goods are to be resolved in the concrete. The specification of such concrete solutions must occur within the moral context. That is to say, it must occur through the responsible use of freedom. This approach introduced a strong emphasis on the developmental and dynamic character of rights, an emphasis which was new to the tradition with Pius XII. It remained for his successors to work out the full implications of this innovation.

JOHN XXIII: HUMAN RIGHTS AND SOCIAL INTERDEPENDENCE

The brief years that John XXIII was pope (1958–1963) were watershed years for the Roman Catholic human rights tradition. The candor, optimism and sense of humor of this transparently Christian man endeared him to the whole world. These same qualities were the source of John XXIII's sensitivity to both the beauties and the pains of the human struggle of this world. His attentiveness to the richness of this complex struggle led him to open the way for innovation and development in the Catholic human rights tradition. John XXIII's decision to convoke the Second Vatican Council arose from his awareness of the need for a thorough re-evaluation of the role of the Catholic Church in the modern world. In response to the growing influence of the Communist party in Italy, John XXIII was willing to go well beyond his predecessors in raising the question of whether such movements might not "contain elements that are positive and deserving of approval" even though they are rooted in "false philosophical teachings." [63] His international experience in Vatican diplomacy had given him first-hand knowledge of the precariousness of international peace. He also perceived that the developments since the Second World War which had led to the promulgation of the U.N. Universal Declaration of Human Rights presented the Church with an opportunity to draw from its tradition and simultaneously to address issues of international peace and justice in a most contemporary language. In seizing this opportunity in *Pacem in Terris* he not only changed the image of the Church to outsiders, but also launched an important process of internal development within the Church's social teaching itself.[64]

John XXIII's 1961 encyclical *Mater et Magistra* outlined the reasons which made a new perspective on social morality necessary. Innovations such as atomic energy and automation were transforming the technological basis of the moral life of society. A whole series of new forms of social legislation was involving government in areas of life previously considered private. Levels of education and political participation were rising. Colonized and newly independent nations were increasing both the range and seriousness of their claims to self-determination, while at the same time there was a growing awareness of the need for international co-operation and organization.[65] All of these changes pointed to the conclusion that "One of the principal characteristics of our time is the multiplication of social relationships, that is, a daily more complex interdependence of citizens." [66] Society, in other words, is becoming more dense and interlocking. Human interrelations are governed by a highly complex and interrelated set of structures.

The consequence of this complexity is two-fold. First, human freedom is more and more both exercised and limited by social organizations, including government.[67] Second, the process of social complexification threatens to undermine people's confidence in their ability to assume responsibility for their own lives. This process thus brings into question the transcendence of persons by threatening to subordinate them to the dynamics of social organization and government.[68]

It is within this analytic context that *Mater et Magistra* proposed the fundamental value of human dignity once again. As was pointed out earlier in the chapter,[69] John XXIII reaffirmed that the human person is "the foundation, cause and end" of all social institutions. The distinctive note in John's affirmation of this traditional principle was his continual emphasis on the fact that human dignity can only exist within a consciously developed context of human interdependence.[70] His belief that persons can avoid becoming entirely instrumentalized by complex social organization depends on the affirmation of the possibility of developing structures which will enable interdependent persons *together* to control these processes.[71] Consequently, the call of human dignity as a moral demand now addresses human beings *in association* in a significantly more important way than was pointed out by previous papal documents.

John XXIII argued that the social processes which threaten to instrumentalize persons are in fact the products of human agency. This agency, however, is shared among many individual persons. This aggregative form of social agency was stressed in a new way by John XXIII. He stated,

actually, increased complexity of social life by no means

> results from a blind drive of natural forces. Indeed, . . . it is the creation of free men who are so disposed to act by nature as to be responsible for what they do.[72]

Thus response to the claims of human dignity is more clearly linked to the protection of the common good of all persons in John XXIII's encyclicals.

Mater et Magistra defines the common good as "the sum total of those conditions of social living, whereby men are enabled more fully and more readily to achieve their own perfection." [73] The common good is here described primarily in structural terms. It is not a summation of the goods of individual citizens, but a set of social conditions which facilitate the realization of personal good by individuals. These conditions are themselves social realities. They are structural and organizational. Thus in a significantly new emphasis within the tradition John XXIII moved toward a definition of human dignity in social and structural terms. This does not mean that he reversed the view that society is for man rather than man for society, a view which remains one of the continuities of the tradition. The new approach derives from the recognition that: 1) human dignity is always supported, conditioned and limited by the forms of social life within which it is found; 2) all arguments about the foundation of morality must take this social context of dignity into consideration as one of their starting points; and 3) the moral response to the claim of the worth of persons will be more and more mediated through social structures, even "in the more intimate aspects of personal life." [74]

The conclusions to be drawn from this line of argument are relatively unsystematized in *Mater et Magistra*. Two years later, in 1963, John XXIII issued *Pacem in Terris,* certainly the most acclaimed of modern papal documents. It is also the most systematic of the modern papal statements on social and political questions. Borrowing the language of the U.N. Universal Declaration, it elaborated a theory of human rights as a framework for international and national peace. *Pacem in Terris* is organized around the most basic principle of Catholic social thought, the dignity of the person. In John XXIII's words:

> Any human society, if it is to be well ordered and productive, must lay down as a foundation this principle, namely, that every human being is a person, that is, his nature is endowed with intelligence and free will. Indeed, precisely because he is a person he has rights and obligations flowing directly and simultaneously from his very nature. And as these rights are universal and inviolable so they cannot in any way be surrendered.[75]

The importance of *Pacem in Terris* lies primarily in its systematic treatment of the consequences of this basic moral norm in highly organized societies and in the world as a whole. It specifies the claims of human dignity in relations between persons, in relations between individuals and public authority within the state, in relations between nations, and in relations among all nations in the international community. The encyclical reiterates Pius XII's view that respect for dignity can occur only within a "community of morally responsible citizens." It reemphasizes *Mater et Magistra's* stress on the fact that human dignity is internally conditioned by human interdependence, an interdependence which exists both within national borders and across them. The rights which protect human dignity, therefore, are the rights of persons *in* community. They are neither exclusively the rights of individuals against the community nor are they the rights of the community against the individual.

Pacem in Terris develops these themes by a careful discussion of the correspondence between rights and duties. To the moral claims which arise from human dignity there correspond duties and responsibilities of society. To every human right there corresponds the duty that this right be respected by the subject of the right himself or herself, by other individual persons and by society. As *Pacem in Terris* puts it:

> Since men are social by nature they are meant to live with others and work for one another's welfare. A well-ordered society requires that men recognize and observe their mutual rights and duties. It also demands that each contribute generously to the establishment of a civic order in which

> rights and duties are more sincerely and effectively acknowledged and secured.[76]

These duties or responsibilities are the responses called for by the dignity of the person in society. They are the result of the interdependence of persons upon one another. And because not only the claims of dignity but also the duties of responsible citizens are essentially personal, they are, in the primary instance, to be exercised in freedom.[77]

Thus the single foundational norm of respect for human dignity led John XXIII to understand both civil-political rights and social-economic rights within a single integrated theoretical framework. In line with the discussion of social complexification in *Mater et Magistra, Pacem in Terris* maintains that the protection and coordination of human rights are increasingly a task which calls for organized action within society as a whole.[78] This implies that social rights are becoming increasingly important. Though governmental action cannot be the sole guarantee of human rights because the complexity of the forms of human interdependence is greater than the flexibility of law, it remains indispensable for the protection of all rights. The action of the state, however, must be constantly checked and reevaluated against the human rights and human dignity it is to protect.[79]

Pacem in Terris gives the most complete and systematic list of these human rights in the modern Catholic tradition. The rights it affirms have been assembled from those mentioned and defended in the previous documents of the tradition. Because of its new perspective on the importance of social institutions and organization, the encyclical has also considerably enlarged the domain of rights. It is a domain which includes both those rights stressed by the liberal democratic tradition and those emphasized by socialists. Its foundation, however, is vastly more stable than the political compromise struck at by the United Nations. Among those goods which *Pacem in Terris* views as due in right to all human beings are the following:

Rights related to *life* and an adequate *standard of living* are the rights to life, bodily integrity, food, clothing, shelter, rest, medical care, necessary social services, security in case of sickness, unemployment, widowhood, old age or unemployment.

As rights concerning *moral and cultural values* the encyclical lists the rights to respect for one's person, to one's good reputation, to freedom of communication, to the pursuit of art, to be informed truthfully; the rights to share in the benefits of culture, to a basic education and to higher education in keeping with the level of development of one's country.

Rights in the area of *religious activity* include the rights to honor God in accord with one's conscience, to practice religion publicly and privately.

In the area of *family* life are the rights to choose one's state of life, that is, to set up a family, with equal rights for men and women, or to choose not to found a family. Also included are the rights to the economic, social, cultural and moral conditions which are necessary for the support of family life, and the prior right of parents to educate their children.

Economic rights include the right to work, the rights to humane working conditions, to appropriate participation in the management of an economic enterprise, to a just wage, to own property within the limits established by social duties.

The encyclical also affirms the rights of *assembly* and *association,* the right to organize societies according to the aim of the members, and the right to organize groups for the purpose of securing goods which the individual cannot attain alone.

All persons have the rights of *freedom of movement* and residence, and to internal and external migration when there is just reason for it.

Political rights include the rights to participate in public affairs and to juridical protection of all one's human rights.[80]

This list of human rights is a systematic recapitulation of the rights claims made by the tradition since Leo XIII. Since 1878 the tradition had been engaged in a process of grappling with a whole range of social, economic and political problems which were threatening the dignity of the person. The response of the Church to these threats had been at times forceful and direct, at times hesitant and indirect. The Church's own institutional interests and its traditional roots in both pre-modern thought and pre-modern European society were the chief causes of hesitancy. The

Church's acknowledgement of the importance of civil and political rights was less rapid than that of European liberalism. Its understanding of the institutional conditions necessary for the protection of social and economic rights developed less rapidly than was the case in socialist movements. Nonetheless, because of a not entirely fortuitous convergence of the demands of institutional interest, intellectual tradition and social conditions, the Roman Catholic tradition was led to respond to the threats to human dignity in a more integrated way than either liberal democracy or Marxism had done. As each of these threats was addressed, different dimensions of the human personality and different types of activity in society were recognized as essential expressions of human worth.

The advance contained in *Pacem in Terris* is its attempt to show that there has been a logic operating throughout the development of the tradition which links these rights together and prevents them from disintegrating into a jumble of *ad hoc* claims. This logic has not unfolded in mathematical or relentlessly linear fashion. It is, however, clearly discernible in historical retrospect. The thread which ties all these rights together is the fundamental norm of human dignity. Human dignity is not an abstract or ethereal reality but is realized in concrete conditions of personal, social, economic and political life. The history of the papal teaching has been a process of discovering and identifying these conditions of human dignity. These conditions are called human rights. Also, these different conditions of dignity are interrelated with each other through the social and political structures of society. The preservation of the worth of the person does not depend simply on the fulfillment of the basic needs of individuals and the protection of their basic freedoms. Rather, the institutions of social and political power must be "ordered" or structured in a way which makes the protection of personal dignity possible. *Pacem in Terris* formulates these positive social and institutional claims in a series of rights at once both personal, social and institutional. They are claims that must be addressed by both the national and international communities.

The central problem raised by *Mater et Magistra* was that of relating the dignity and freedom of the individual to the complexifying social structures of a politically and technologically interdependent world. In *Pacem in Terris* John XXIII has gone a long way toward specifying the shape of this relationship with his charter of human rights. *Pacem in Terris,* however, was not the final word of the tradition on this problem. John recognized that the task of protecting human worth in its social context "is marked by a pronounced dynamism." [81] This dynamism is evident in a society in which the patterns of interdependence between persons are constantly shifting. It remained for the most recent documents of the tradition to develop principles for specifying the relationship between personal dignity and social conditions in a milieu characterized by increasing awareness of human historicity.

The Second Vatican Council: Personal Dignity in History

Two years after the publication of *Pacem in Terris,* during its last session in 1965, the Second Vatican Council approved and promulgated two documents which carry the Catholic understanding of human dignity and human rights a step further. The *Pastoral Constitution on the Church in the Modern World (Gaudium et Spes)* and the *Declaration on Religious Liberty (Dignitatis Humanae Personae)* were the two most significant statements of the Council related to questions of social morality. The primary contribution of the first of these documents was its innovative discussion of the religious basis of Christian ethical concern. This theological development will be at the focal point of the next chapter. *Gaudium et Spes* does, however, make a number of significant contributions to the discussion of the foundations of a theory of human rights. These will be reviewed briefly here. *Dignitatis Humanae* is concerned with a very particular and important human right: the right to religious liberty. But in the course of its treatment of religious liberty it appeals to a number of more general conceptions of the moral life which are also important in this context.

The Council's most important contribution to the human

rights tradition was its important new acknowledgement that the demands of human dignity are historically conditioned ones. The historical and developing character of human personhood is repeatedly affirmed in *Gaudium et Spes*. The Council's understanding of the relation between the transcendental worth of persons and the historical realization of this worth leads it to conclude that the full implications of dignity of the person cannot be known or affirmed apart from the concrete conditions of an historical epoch.

The same social, technological, economic and political developments which stimulated *Mater et Magistra*'s emphasis on the complex interdependencies of social, economic and political life are interpreted as evidence for the importance of historicity in *Gaudium et Spes*. The issues raised by this evidence can be stated as follows. If persons in society possess a transcendental worth, then the structures of social organization are confronted with claims to serve and protect this personal dignity. The precise content of these claims, however, is historically conditioned. Thus it is impossible to specify the conditions of human dignity *a priori*. Any justification of particular claims which would grant them the status of rights involves a measure of historical judgment. Any appeal to the nature of the human person which is used to justify rights claims must take into account the fact that this nature is structured and conditioned both historically and socially.[82] The recognition of historicity as an essential characteristic of human personhood thus threatens to undermine human rights by relativizing them. It also threatens to relegate human rights claims to mere expressions of cultural and ideological bias.

Gaudium et Spes does not give a systematically unified response to this newly recognized problem. However, two things are clear in the document. First, the challenge of historicity to the traditional notions of dignity and rights is recognized. And second, the Council reaffirms and clarifies the validity of the tradition's view that moral obligation is not simply a matter of cultural bias or prejudice. In some places this reaffirmation is made by restating the matter within the conceptual framework provided by earlier documents, in others it is shaped by a significantly new perspective.

The newer perspective adopted by the Council has several dimensions. First, the recognition of the problem is evident in the introductory articles of *Gaudium et Spes*. Here the Council embarked upon the task which John XXIII had recommended to it, that of scrutinizing the "signs of the times." Especially important among the characteristics of our age is a prevalent sense of anxiousness about "the place and role of man in the universe, about the meaning of his individual and collective strivings, and about the ultimate destiny of reality and of humanity." [83] This anxiety is the result of a loss of confidence in the lasting worth of human projects and ideas. Our age is a period of genuine "social and cultural transformation," triggered by the social, political and technological creations of human intelligence. It is an age characterized by continual discovery of new possibilities for social life and new interpretations of the underlying structures of social interaction. But it is also a time in which people increasingly recognize that their desires and decisions are deeply shaped by their social context. This recognition threatens to bring many to a state "paralyzed by uncertainty". Historical relativity, anxiety over the growing power of new forms of social and psychological slavery, and moral uncertainty go hand in hand. The unity of the human race is threatened by the fracturing of the meaning structure by which persons understand their lives into "diverse ideological systems." [84]

Gaudium et Spes develops its distinctively new viewpoint on the ethical function of the norm of human dignity within this framework of modern uncertainty and anxiety. From an examination of the sociological and cultural situation, the Constitution moves inward to the personal and spiritual impact of these changes. The tensions which are experienced in contemporary culture are not simply material contradictions explainable by means of physical or mechanical analogies. The tensions are a result of a conflict within human existence itself. This conflict is characterized as one between the drive of the human spirit toward a value worthy of absolute commitment and the shifting and limited values of historical existence. In the words of the Constitution:

> The truth is that the imbalances under which the modern world labors are linked with that more basic imbalance rooted in the heart of man. For in man himself many elements wrestle with one another. Thus, on the one hand, as a creature he experiences his limitations in a multitude of ways. On the other, he feels himself to be boundless in his desires and summoned to a higher life.[85]

Historical awareness brings this inner spiritual dynamic to the forefront of the Council's discussion of the place of the person both within the cosmos and in history. The discovery of change brings the limited and conditioned quality of the structures of human existence into clear light. At the same time this discovery releases consciousness from its submersion within these limits and conditions, bringing to light the transcendence of the person.

This simultaneous presence within the person of the sense of historical limitation and the drive to transcendence becomes the focus of the new ethical treatment of personal dignity in the Constitution. This tension can have two undesirable kinds of results. The quest for transcendence could be focused on an historically limited value in a way which absolutizes this value. The result would be idolatry and enslavement.[86] On the other hand, a complete or premature withdrawal from historical engagement in the name of pure transcendence is also a temptation. The Constitution recognizes both of these tendencies as permanent aspects of human experience in an historically developing world. They are at the root of human sinfulness. When both are present to consciousness persons recognize themselves as "split" and divided.[87]

The tension within the person described here, however, is both the positive source of the personal ability to make history and the result of this ability. More accurately, it is impossible to imagine a being conscious of his own participation in historical growth and change who would not be subject to such a tension. Historical existence demands the presence of the two poles of this tension: the pole of involvement in the limited and conditioned on the one hand and the pole of transcendence into the new, the unlimited and the absolute on the other. It is on this basis that the Council's acceptance of historicity leads it to an unequivocal reaffirmation of the dignity of the human person. Finite beings in which the tensions of historicity are not present are dumb, brute, unconscious—in short, they are things. Beings in which such tensions are present are human persons. They are neither things nor pieces in a social machine. Neither are they gods.

Within this framework it becomes evident that the limits and conditions of historical existence are not the enemies of human dignity. Rather the limited conditions of nature and history are the context within which personal dignity is realized. The human body and its emersion in the whole world of nature, the concreteness of personal relationships, and the structures of social organization are all essential for the preservation of man's historical life as a person. They limit and condition the human personality. They are not, however, to be understood primarily as constrictions of the expansiveness of the human spirit. They can become constrictive and oppressive when they are not properly ordered, but in their primary structure, bodiliness, interpersonal relationships and social organization are positive possibilities in and through which human dignity is realized.[88]

The Pastoral Constitution goes one step further and affirms that these structures for the realization of human dignity are of two types: some relate with immediacy to the "innermost nature" of the person, others change through history as the result of the decisions of persons, groups and societies.[89] In the first category *Gaudium et Spes* includes such forms of human interrelationship as the family and the political community. To deny persons the right to family life or political participation in some form is to deny an essential dimension of the human personality. The precise form which these rights will take in the concrete, however, can only be determined in the context of an historical analysis of the patterns and institutions of social life.

The present historical situation has intensified the importance of the essentially social nature of persons. A deepened appreciation of social interdependence and a recognition of its widening range of influence in human life is evident in an important passage from *Gaudium et Spes* which echoes *Mater et Magistra:*

> In our era, for various reasons, reciprocal ties and mutual dependencies increase day by day and give rise to a variety of associations and organizations, both public and private. This development, which is called socialization, while certainly not without its dangers, brings with it many advantages with respect to consolidating and increasing the qualities of the human person and safeguarding his rights.[90]

In this statement a fundamental methodological approach to the determination of the scope of valid human rights claims in contemporary societies is revealed. The permanent demands of human dignity and the historical form these demands now take are not viewed as if they were two levels or planes running parallel to each other. Rather in this passage a permanent characteristic of human nature—its essentially social character—is realized in the historically conditioned form of "socialization" or increased interdependence. It would be a grave error to neglect the fact that social existence is a naturally given quality of human persons in any historical era. To do so would be to separate the forms of societal organization from their essential relationship to human personhood and dignity. At the same time, to attempt to realize this natural sociability in our era without taking cognizance of the massively increased interdependence of persons would be to fail to heed the claims which human dignity makes within the particularity and uniqueness of this historical period.

The interpenetration of the permanent and the historical dimensions of human existence is evident in the increasing ability of persons to reshape the limits of human life previously considered unchangeable. It is also notable in the intensified mutual dependence between persons on all levels of social organization, and in the increasing frequency and wider scope of legitimate government intervention.[91] The result of this view of changed social conditions is the conclusion that the fundamental moral obligation to respect human dignity is not to be defined in permanently fixed institutional patterns.

The determination of the justified claims of human dignity within this framework is thus a most complex task. The Council offers a number of negative criteria which can serve to make the demands of the task somewhat lighter. Human behavior must not deny the goodness of the body by treating it as something separate from human personhood. The exercise of human intelligence brings greater dignity to persons, so the expansion of the educational and cultural opportunities of persons is called for wherever this is possible. Human dignity can only be realized in faithfulness to one's conscience. The organization of action in freedom rather than through coercion is an essential characteristic of human personhood in society.[92]

Gaudium et Spes thus suggests a fruitful way to combine the traditional view of human rights as rooted in human nature with modern historical consciousness. There are domains of human existence which cannot be suppressed without oppressing human beings. These include respect for the bodily, interpersonal, social-political, economic and cultural dimensions of human existence. Because of the increasing interdependence of persons the means to this respect must be more and more through the organized action of communities and of society as a whole. Thus from the perspective of the Council, social, economic and cultural rights, defined in relation to historical conditions, assume a new place of importance in the Catholic human rights tradition.

The Council's Declaration on Religious Freedom, *Dignitatis Humanae Personae* was also a major contribution to the developing social ethical tradition of modern Catholicism. The Declaration's chief purpose was to bring Catholic teaching abreast of modern Western thought on the right to religious liberty and to overcome the historical lag between Catholic and Western constitutional thinking on this subject. In rethinking this one right, the Council brought Catholic social thought into a new relationship with the entire Western liberal tradition. Like *Gaudium et Spes, Dignitatis Humanae* frames its doctrinal position with an analysis of the moral problematic of contemporary society. Article 1 acknowledges and affirms the increasing consciousness of human dignity and personal responsibility which characterizes contemporary humanity. Article 8 notes the ambiguity of this new consciousness. Human personhood and responsibility are simultaneously more threatened and more esteemed than in previous history. John Courtney Murray, who is well known as one of the chief drafters of the Declaration, describes the framework this way: "The Council calls attention to the paradox of the moment. Freedom today is threatened; freedom today is itself a threat." [93] Pietro Pavan, a social ethicist who also participated in the formulation of the Declaration and in the drafting of John XXIII's encyclicals as well, is in agreement with this view of the way the problem treated by the Declaration is posed. He finds its context to be the issue which dominates John XXIII's encyclicals and *Gaudium et Spes,* namely, the tension between socialization and personalization.[94]

In *Dignitatis Humanae* we find laid bare in quite explicit terms, therefore, the principle of doctrinal development within continuity which has controlled the modern Catholic social teaching. The strains created within modern society by the simultaneous threat to human dignity and responsibility and the increasing power and range of human creativity have driven the tradition to a deepened recognition of its own principle of dynamic continuity. This principle is that of the dignity of the responsible person in society. It is brought to the clear light of day when *Dignitatis Humanae* states that the Council "intends to develop the doctrine of recent Popes on the inviolable rights of the human person and on the constitutional order of society."[95] As is the case with doctrinal developments in general, however, theological, philosophical and social challenges to the undeveloped insight have served to clarify, refine and advance both understanding and expression. Murray summarized the process within the tradition:

> In no other conciliar document is it so explicitly stated that the intention of the Council is to "develop" Catholic doctrine. This is significant, since it is an avowal that the tradition of the Church is a tradition of progress in understanding the truth. The basic truth here is the concept of the "citizen" as stated by Pius XII—the man who "feels within himself a consciousness of his own personality, of his duties, and of his rights, joined with a respect for the freedom of others" (Christmas Discourse, 1945). This conception, as the declaration will say, is deeply rooted both in the Christian tradition and the tradition of reason. In recent times, it was Leo

> XIII (in "Rerum Novarum") who first began to move it, as it were, to the forefront of Catholic social teaching. Piux XII continued this development, drawing out the implications of the dignity of man in terms of his duties and rights. He also brought forward the correlative truth that the primary function of government is to acknowledge, protect, vindicate, and facilitate the exercise of the rights of man. Both of these truths were taken up by John XXIII, chiefly in *Pacem in Terris,* in which they are given an almost systematic form of statement.[96]

We find in *Dignitatis Humanae,* therefore, an important key to the problem of the foundation, interrelation and institutionalization of human rights. Responsible use of freedom defines the very nature of social morality. The definition of the content of this responsibility must occur within the context of changing cultural and social structures. Thus human rights are rights *within society*. They are both negative immunities and positive entitlements. And, as *Dignitatis Humanae* affirms in continuity with the earlier documents, it is the function of government to intervene to assure that all the rights and duties of citizens are brought into the harmony of a moral order, thus assuring public peace.[97] The state must protect freedom, and to this end freedom may be regulated. It may not regulate in order to assure that a particular ideology, whether religious or secular, becomes normative for all in society. The focus is on persons in interaction, not on theories or religions seeking adherents. The concern of the argument is, in short, for the person and his or her freedom to act in society. The state may not substitute itself for the responsible citizen. It may regulate, which is to say it may order, human interaction. For *Dignitatis Humanae,* as for Piux XII, order is an ordering of freedom. Only thus is it possible to understand the common root of both personal and social rights and to see their essential interrelationship with each other.

Paul VI: Integral Development

The new emphases in Vatican II's understanding of the foundations of human rights have borne their first fruits in the writings of Paul VI. Since he became pope in 1963, Paul VI has issued two major statements on social morality, the encyclical *Populorum Progressio* (1967) and the Apostolic Letter commemorating the eightieth anniversary of *Rerum Novarum, Octogesima Adveniens* (1971). Both of Paul VI's social statements begin with an acknowledgement that they belong to a new period of self-understanding within the Roman Catholic tradition.

The Council's careful discussion of both the historical and social nature of human dignity has given *Populorum Progressio* and *Octogesima Adveniens* a focus that is genuinely new. Pope Paul's social statements are shaped throughout by consciousness of the historicity of social institutions. They are also dominated by concern with transnational and international patterns of human interdependence. The problems of economic development, international economic relationships, and, above all, the poverty of developing nations are the central concerns of these documents. These two documents are also fully aware of the ideological pluralism which reigns in discussions of how to address these massive problems. The problem of the conflict of interpretations and values in social and political development have thus recently become major themes in Catholic social thought. The crisp, lucid and affirmative style of *Pacem in Terris'* discussion of human rights has been replaced by a more complex and tentative mode of analysis in *Populorum Progressio* and *Octogesima Adveniens*. This has led at least one commentator to raise the question of whether *Populorum Progressio* really marks an abandonment of the main thread of the Catholic rights tradition.[98] The issue which these documents raise, however, is more fundamental than this. The question is whether the historical consciousness and social interdependence stressed at the Council force us to abandon all talk of human rights as a form of discourse which is individualistic and naive about the reality of ideological conflict.

Populorum Progressio gives a negative answer to this question. Its reasoning is built around the complex concept of "integral development." The human personality is multifacited. The protection of human dignity, therefore, requires respect for the multiple social, economic, intellectual, interpersonal and religious conditions of personal development. As *Populorum Progressio* puts it, "To be genuine, growth must be integral, it must clearly provide for the progress of each individual and of the whole man." [99] The development of the person is properly regarded as the realization of the human potential for the knowledge, responsibility and freedom which are constitutive of personhood. It includes actualization of the human capacities for love, friendship, and at the highest level of human realization, prayer and contemplation.[100] It calls for those minimum levels of economic well being which are essential to the realization of personal worth.[101]

All of this, of course, can be achieved only in society and through social collaboration. It can occur only in a society which structures itself to protect and promote the realization of these values through its institutions. Thus, in the document's words "This perfecting of the human person is to be considered a summary, so to speak, of our obligations." [102] The normative standard of integral development therefore *includes* all those personal and social rights which have been set forward in previous phases of the tradition. The content of these rights and their interrelationships with each other, however, will only be judged accurately when they are viewed in integral relationship with each other. *Populorum Progressio* does not regard economic well-being simply as a minimum standard which is extrinsic to the development and dignity of the person. This kind of dualism is both foreign to the concept of integral development and unresponsive to the historically concrete situations of the vast number of poor persons who are the concern of the encyclical. As Quentin Lauer has pointed out, *Populorum Progressio* makes a significant advance in the way the tradition affirms the importance of material well-being for the realization of human dignity.[103] Material well-being is not simply instrumental in value. It is not a means of dignified life. It is, rather, *integral* to the standard of all moral value, human dignity. Paul VI is clear, of course, that the economic dimension is not the sole criterion of genuine development. He is equally clear that the improvement of material conditions is an essential aspect of this development. Persons quite legitimately seek "to do more, know more and have more in order to be more." [104] Possession of economic well-being, when properly coordinated with the other aspects of development, is thus perceived by the encyclical as a positive value directly related to human dignity.

From this it is evident that the use of the standard of integral development to determine the concrete demands of human dignity will involve complex and dialectically related considerations. The development of all the potentialities of human personhood cannot be achieved through a single decision or action by an individual person. Some balancing of the values and setting of priorities will be necessary. For example, the development of individual persons is linked with that of others through the priorities and structural relationships which are institutionalized in the economy and in political life. The use of the standard of integral development therefore demands that the problem of both real and potential conflict of values and social systems be dealt with.

Populorum Progressio acknowledges that conflict between different values, all regarded as dimensions of integral development, does indeed exist in the present situation of world society. Inequality and conflict between rich and poor are characteristic of the industrialized nations. This situation is even more pronounced between nations. Also, conflict is characteristic of the relations between various social classes, most painfully in the poor countries.[105] Such conflicts are not simply the results of bad will on the part of those who are involved in them, though this factor is not overlooked by the encyclical. They are also the result of inequities which have been crystallized in the institutions of society.

It is clear that *Populorum Progressio* believes that the resolution of conflicts between different aspects of the fundamental norm of development in dignity is not an illusory goal. The resolution can occur, however, only if the conflict is regarded within a moral context. That is, it must be placed within a context in which genuine claims to respect the dignity, needs and freedoms of others are experienced. The resolution of conflicts depends on an active, responsive and mutual respect for the dignity of persons. It is for this reason that *Populorum Progressio* strongly affirms that there can be no integral development which is not based on mutual respect: "The complete development of the individual must be joined with that of the human race and must be accomplished by mutual effort." [106] This relationship of mutuality is conceived, in continuity with both Pius XII and John XXIII, as specified in certain concrete moral demands—human rights and duties. Human rights, therefore, are expressions of the more fundamental moral experience of human solidarity. Whether these rights be negative immunities or positive entitlements they presuppose that persons recognize that they are bound together in a moral community of mutual interdependence.

It is within this context that *Populorum Progressio's* complex statement of the relation of the different dimensions of integral development to each other should be understood. It will be helpful to cite it at length:

> These must be said to be dwelling in less human living conditions: first those who are hard pressed by such destitution as to lack either the minimum subsistence necessary for life or who are almost crushed by moral deficiency which they have brought upon themselves by excessive self-love; secondly those who are oppressed by social structures which abuses of ownership or power, exploitation of workers or unjust transactions have created. Contrariwise the following indicate with sufficient clarity that more human living conditions have been achieved: first the passing from destitution to the possession of necessities, winning the struggle against social ills, broader knowledge, acquisition of culture; secondly increased esteem for the dignity of others, an inclination to the spirit of poverty, cooperation for the common good, the will for peace; then acknowledgement by man of the highest good, the recognition of God Himself, the author and end of these blessings; finally and especially faith, the gift of God, accepted by men of good will, and unity in the love of Christ who has called us to share as sons the life of the living God, the Father of all men.[107]

This paragraph, in its rather awkward phrasing and strained parallelisms, is attempting to spell out the encyclical's understanding of the method of conflict resolution. The list of conditions given here is not a strict hierarchy of values. Neither is it a proposal of a program by which various values should be striven for sequentially through time. For example, one can hardly imagine Paul VI saying that religious dimensions of human development can or should be realized only after the struggle against social ills has been won. But he does contend that there is a correlation between the destitution of some and the moral deficiency of others. Oppression by social structures is linked with the absence of respect for human dignity. It is thus that *Populorum Progressio* can draw a firm conclusion that the development of persons must simultaneously include progress on the material level and greater realization of the higher values of human existence. Human dignity can only be respected and realized within a society when the essentially moral call to mutual interdependence is heeded. This does not imply that all the desires and freedoms of all people will be realized in an unlimited way in such a society. Rather, *Populorum Progressio* argues that when human dignity is treated with mutual respect, a society which is *morally developed* will be realized. The economic development of some persons and the moral development of others are systematically interlinked in the integral moral development of the whole society. In this important sense, but in this sense only, will conflict be resolved.[108]

This viewpoint leads to the conclusion that the domain of the morally fitting and the domain of possible realizations of the potential of the human personality are not coextensive, even though they are closely interrelated. For example, unlimited increase in wealth and technological development, through genuine possibilities in advanced industrial societies, must be limited by the needs of developing nations. Conflict cannot be resolved in a way consistent with the dignity of persons unless the distinction between the development of a moral community and the unfettered pursuit of individual or group development is recognized. Without such differentiation the equal dignity of persons will easily be subordinated to a partial or discriminatory pattern of development.

This distinction is evident in *Populorum Progressio's* critique of all ideologies which focus exclusively on one dimension of human personality to the exclusion of others. It has become one of the central concerns of *Octogesima Adveniens,* Paul VI's Apostolic Letter of 1971. In this document the presence of conflicting interpretations of social existence has been fully recognized. The document was occasioned by the urgent need to clarify the political relationship between the Church and governments or movements operating on clear ideological principles. Most urgently the relation between the Church and Marxists in Latin America and Eastern Europe needed clarification. *Octogesima Adveniens* is critical of those forms of both Marxism and liberalism which programatically deny the fullness of integral development whether on ideological or strategic grounds. Each of these political and economic systems, if raised to the level of a complete social program, denies dimensions of personal and social development which are integral to human dignity. They solve the problem of the conflict of values prematurely by denying social recognition to some of the competing dimensions of the person.[109]

Octogesima Adveniens, however, makes an important distinction between the exclusive and ideological use of the values defended by liberalism and Marxism and their use as theoretical explanations of *aspects* of integral development. Marxist thought can help to develop a scientific analysis of structural, economic conflict. Liberal thought provides insights into the economic and political means for protecting personal self-determination and initiative. Both visions of how society should be organized, though partial, contain truth. The scientific development of these two major ideologies is "at once indispensable and inadequate for a better discovery of what is human." [110]

Where does this leave the Roman Catholic rights tradition? Has the acknowledgement of historicity and the problem of ideological pluralism and conflict thrown the tradition into the maelstrom of ethical relativism? The answer to this question is a firm negative. The tone of *Octogesima Adveniens* is much less definitive and final than any previous papal document. But all is not left open to debate. The norm of personal dignity remains central. *Octogesima Adveniens* is even optimistic that the present pluralism may bring about a rediscovery of the central foundation of all obligations by the contenders in the conflict of interpretations. Paul VI sees this relativization of ideologies as a possible indication of a new openness to the "concrete transcendence" of Christianity. This concrete transcendence is precisely the dignity of the human person: fully rooted in social and historical conditions, yet always surpassing and judging them. The various social locations of the agents of change as well as the diverse methods of interpretation of social reality will lead to a variety of legitimate options for political action. But the concrete transcendence of human dignity continues to make its claims: minimum conditions of material well-being must be met, freedom is to be defended, but in a way which recognizes the needs and dignity of others, and integral development is impossible apart from human solidarity.[111] The range of governmental action will continue to expand, but it too remains limited in both principle and practice by the dignity of persons.

These principles and the human rights they entail do not constitute a social or political program. They are, however, both minimum standards that must be met by all such programs, and principles which can shape the conscience of responsible agents. They are, in short, norms of discernment.[112] They simultaneously set limits and point the way. They define the sphere of morality, as distinct from other spheres such as the economic or cultural or political. In other words, these principles of discernment are an expression in thought of the reality of human dignity. A society which respects dignity is a society which forms its decisions and policies by them.

THE 1971 SYNOD OF BISHOPS: THE RIGHT TO DEVELOPMENT

The impact of the Second Vatican Council on the Roman Catholic rights tradition was not limited to the changes which it stimulated in papal teaching. One of the most significant results of the Council was the establishment of the international Synod of Bishops. This body is an institutional expression of the Council's recognition of the realities of cultural diversity in both the world and the Church. Its establishment has begun the process of translating into action the Council's commitment to a less centralized form of church organization. In its second session, in 1971, the Synod turned its attention to concerns of special importance to the churches of Africa, Asia and Latin America: the problems of justice and human rights. The results of its deliberations were set down in the document *Justice in the World*. This document is both carefully balanced and aggressively innovative. It incorporates both the strength of the tradition's theory of human dignity and rights, on the one hand, and differentiated understanding of social relationships characteristic of Paul VI's writings on the other.

It does this through a recognition that human dignity implies a constellation of rights which must be understood, not singly, but in dynamic interrelation with each other. This interlocking of rights is most evident in the Synod's affirmation of the existence of "right to development." It defines the right as "a dynamic interpenetration of all those fundamental human rights upon which the aspirations of individuals and nations are based." [113] This right should not be regarded simply as an additional right to be added to the list which can be assembled by a reading of the previous documents. Its emergence clarifies the tradition's understanding of how the content of rights is to be determined. The concrete content of the demands of dignity can only be specified through an analysis of the kinds of relationships which actually govern human interaction. In the words of the Synod:

> The strong drive toward global unity, the unequal distribution which places decisions concerning three-quarters of income, investment and trade in the hands of one-third of the human race, namely the more highly developed part, the insufficiency of merely economic progress, and the new recognition of the material limits of the biosphere—all this makes us aware that in today's world new modes of understanding human dignity are arising.[114]

The import of this statement lies in its suggestion that dignity is not determinable or measurable on a linear scale somehow derived from a scrutiny of the nature of the individual person. The need for new modes of understanding dignity arises from an analysis of predominant institutional patterns of human interaction—economic, political, technological and ecological.

First, the Synod notes that economic interdependence and the delicate ecological balance which binds life with life are primary determinants of the possibility of realizing human dignity. At the same time, however, the advances in the technology of warfare, the rapid increase in population due to medical advances, and the increasing urbanization of the poor have led to a deepening division within society. In this context the document spells out the importance of a relational definition of the demands of dignity. The chief threat to personal dignity in a world of rapid technological growth is that large segments of the population will simply be excluded from any active participation in shaping the social patterns which provide the context of their lives. The technological divisions within society

> constantly give rise to great numbers of "marginal" persons, ill-fed, inhumanly housed, illiterate and deprived of political power as well as of the suitable means of acquiring responsibility and moral dignity.[115]

Marginalization or lack of participation thus becomes a primary criterion for judging if human dignity is being violated. Lack of adequate nourishment, housing, education and political self-determination are seen as a consequence of this lack of participation. The Synod predicts the consequences of a failure to heed the fundamental claim to participation:

> Unless combatted and overcome by social and political action, the influence of the new industrial and technological order favors the concentration of wealth, power and decision making in the hands of a small public or private controlling group. Economic injustice and lack of social participation keep a man from attaining his basic human and civil rights.[116]

Therefore, the relational quality of human dignity is spelled out by the Synod in terms of a fundamental right to participation which integrates all the other rights with each other and provides their operational foundation. Violation of dignity is regarded primarily as lack of influence on and participation in the shaping of the social forces which determine the limits within which human agency is effective.[117] Indeed, the Synod's analysis of present social patterns indicates that this circle of agency is shrinking to the vanishing point for a very large segment of the human race.

The right to development affirmed by the Synod must be understood against the backdrop of this analysis. This right is not an amorphous conflation of other rights which are known through their own independent analytic perspectives. Rather, the right to development, as it is conceptualized by the Synod, is the first specification of the demands of dignity in the present historical situation. Respect for persons demands active participation in the process of social change and development. Such participation is the condition for the realization of all human potentialities. None of these potentialities can or will be realized as long as persons remain in a condition of extreme marginalization and powerlessness.

The right to development is in a sense a comparative right. Its concrete content can only be discovered by regarding the individual person within his or her social context and in relation to other persons. Quantitative measures of caloric or protein intake, units of housing per capita, annual income, doctors per capita, etc., are most important in the determination of the minimum standards for human dignity. But the Synod document does not base its conclusions about the right to development solely on a comparison of the figures on *these* variables for different social groups. The comparative nature of the right should not be regarded as strictly quantitative or economic. The most significant question to be asked in making the social comparison is not "How much more food or housing or money does John have than Juan does?" Such quantitative comparisons, precisely as comparisons, are relevant only because extremes of quantitative inequality are both causes and manifestations of an exclusion of some persons from the processes which protect and promote the active expression of human dignity. It is this qualitative comparative standard of participation which can be used to determine when human dignity is being supported or violated by complex social structures. Thus the right to development, as the precondition of all other rights, is given specificity as the right to participation. The more quantitative claims expressed in the economic notion of development have their roots in the claims to participation. In the words of the Synod:

> It is impossible to conceive true progress without recognizing the necessity—within the political system chosen—of a development composed both of economic growth and participation; and the necessity too of an increase in wealth implying as well social progress by the entire community as it overcomes regional imbalance and islands of prosperity. Participation constitutes a right which is to be applied in the economic and in the social and political field.[118]

The right to development thus implies that all other rights are expressions of the claims of the person to be a self-determining agent, that is, they are expressions of claims to be a participant in the social, economic and political process.

This framework for the analysis of the claims of human dignity avoids the pitfall of relativizing out of existence the specific list of rights which was worked out in *Pacem in Terris*. The specificity of *Pacem in Terris* is not present in *Justice in the World,* but the concern for establishing firm criteria for judging respect for personal dignity is both evident and successful. The right to development is the norm which has led to the Synod's affirmation of a number of more particular rights: the right of self-determination, the right to participate in the formation of economic, social and political structures, the right to the preservation of one's cultural identity, the rights to religious freedom, due process and a fair trial, the rights to life and bodily integrity, the right to the presentation of truth in communications media, the right to freedom from manipulation by images presented by the media, and the right to education.[119] In a significant new emphasis, the Synod document stresses the importance that human rights be fully respected in the internal structures and procedures of the Church. In this context it affirms the right to a just wage, the right to participation, the rights of women, the rights to freedom of expression and thought, the right to due process of law.[120] All of these specific rights are integrally linked with each other. The way in which they are to be secured can only be by acknowledgement of their interlocking nature. The forms of political and social structure through which they are to be secured are not predetermined in advance. The overcoming of marginalization through participation, however, will be characteristic of every social and legal system which is in accord with the dignity of the human person. Though *Justice in the World* lacks the systematic approach to rights found in *Pacem in Terris,* it provides a social analysis and a fundamental normative vision of the present situation which point the way to the implementation of Pope John's charter of rights.

Development and Differentiation of the Theory of Rights

The history of modern Catholicism's understanding of the ethical foundations of human rights has been a complex one. It has developed under the crisscrossing historical pressures of political events, economic realities, ideological conflicts, and the institutional interests of the Church itself. Thus the Church's teaching on human rights has not been set forth with the lean lines of a rigorous moral argument. Nonetheless, an outline of what such an argument would look like can be constructed from the elements and trajectory of the tradition.

First, our review of this history shows the truth of John XXIII's claim that the fundamental and dominant concern of the tradition has been single and clear: the preservation and promotion of the dignity of the human person. The effort to affirm the overriding value of persons is the unifying thread through all the documents we have reviewed. This dignity is a characteristic of all persons—the ground from which emerge all moral claims, all rights, all duties. The preservation and promotion of human dignity are the sum and substance of all such claims, rights and duties.

As the Catholic rights tradition understands it, human dignity is as an indicative rather than as an imperative. Human persons *have* dignity. They *are* sacred and precious. In this sense, dignity is not granted to persons by the ethical activity of others. Dignity is not bestowed on persons by other persons, by the family or society or the state. Rather the reality of human dignity makes claims on others that it be recognized and respected. The moral imperatives set forth as human rights express the more specific content of these claims. Human dignity, however, is more fundamental than any specific human right. It is the source of all moral principles, not a moral principle itself. Particular human rights can therefore be understood only when they are seen as rooted in this fundamental norm.

Secondly, human dignity is not a concept which derives its meaning from a particular class or genus of human actions. It has reality in all situations, independent of the kinds of actions and relations which give them structure. Dignity is thus a transcendental characteristic of persons. Human persons have a worth which claims respect in every situation and in every type of activity. Dignity is the norm by which the adequacy of all forms of human behavior and all the moral principles which are formulated to guide behavior are to be judged. Human dignity is therefore not primarily a guiding rule or principle which is formulated by and within reflexive human consciousness. It is a concrete reality which exists wherever persons exist. The affirmation of dignity as an ontological characteristic of every human person is present throughout the tradition we have reviewed. Thus the Roman Catholic tradition answers the question of the foundation of human rights with a single phrase: the dignity of the human person.

This transcendental conception of dignity is a paradoxical one, however. Human dignity is an entirely concrete reality. Indeed, the primary referent of the term is not conceptual but existential: concrete existing human beings. At the same time the bare notion of human dignity is nearly empty of meaning. This is so because without further specification the notion of human dignity lacks all reference to particular needs, actions and relationships.

As a transcendental characteristic of persons it is not identical in meaning with the fulfillment of any need, with the freedom for any particular kind of action or with the attainment of any specific kind of relationship. The mistake of both liberal-democratic and Marxist thought has been the identification of a limited domain of human existence with the radical foundation of human rights. In the case of liberal democracy this foundation is limited to human freedom negatively understood. In the case of Marxism, it is contracted by a particular interpretation of class conflict and the means for achieving social change. The Roman Catholic tradition recognizes, however, that a critique of these too limited definitions of human dignity is not enough. Unless the relations between the transcendental worth of the person and the particular material, interpersonal, social and political structures of human existence can be specified, human dignity will become an empty notion. The specification of the concrete conditions for the realization of dignity in action has been the continuing endeavor of the tradition since Leo XIII. This endeavor has produced the Catholic human rights tradition.

The process of identifying the concrete claims of human dignity is necessarily a continuing one. The material conditions, economic patterns and forms of political association in which persons live are continually changing. Human dignity can be protected under diverse social and political arrangements precisely because it is not identified with any of them. The task of identifying the concrete norms of social morality thus demands continual reevaluation of shifting material, social, economic and political conditions in terms of their effects on the lives of persons.

The effort to identify these conditions of dignity has led the Roman Catholic tradition to the affirmation of a number of different human rights. Rights are the conditions for the realization of human worth in action. These human rights concern such diverse human needs as life, food, shelter, sexuality and work. They refer to various domains of freedom and self-determination, such as freedom of expression, association, religion, communication. They concern different kinds of human inter-relation such as the familial, the economic, the political, the cultural and the religious. The various rights set forth in the documents are statements of the claims that arise from the ground of dignity in each of these differentiated areas of need, freedom and relationship.

It is the continuing effort to specify the claims of dignity in each of these areas which has produced the development of the Roman Catholic rights tradition.[121] We can point to several distinct phases in this development. In Leo XIII's economic ethic we find an argument that the material needs must be met to at least a minimal degree if human dignity is to be actively respected in society. Thus he affirmed the rights to food, clothing, shelter, and adequate wages. Ownership of property was seen as an important instrumental means for the protection of these rights. In the political realm Leo XIII saw that the person must be free from domination both by the state and by ruthless employers if his or her transcendental worth is not to be denied in action. In Leo XIII's writings there was a notable tendency to define the conditions of human dignity in terms of negative criteria. Though certainly not individualistic in approach, his encyclicals were primarily concerned to set boundaries which define dignity defensively. Leo's concern that property rights be extended to all is an example of this emphasis. Property protects the individual from the encroachments of the state and of other social groups. Here Leo XIII adopted arguments remarkably similar to those of Locke. He went beyond Locke, however, in his insistance that actual ownership be distributed as widely as possible.

The defensive tendency was even more marked in Leo XIII's continuing support of the hierarchical and traditional ordering of political society. This support was in large measure due to Leo's concern to protect the privileged position of religious authority which was so much a part of the heritage of Christendom. In Leo's view, an organic and hierarchically structured society was a necessary means to the protection of dignity. He viewed the boundaries of such a society like a solid mold into which the precious but fluid element of dignity is poured in order to give it structure and shape. As a generalization which is not without important exceptions, it appears true that for Leo XIII the differentiated conditions for the protection of human dignity are defined in terms of a pre-established societal form. These forms are essential, but they are extrinsic to dignity itself. Thus both the inter-relations between rights and the means for institutionalizing rights are influenced by this taken-for-granted social order. That this is an uneasy generalization is apparent from the implicit thrust toward social and political change present in Leo's understanding of economic rights. For Leo XIII, as for us today, concern for economic rights pointed toward the need for a new kind of institutional and juridical order. We will return to this need in Chapter Four, where the problem of institutional means for dealing with conflicts of rights will be discussed.

In Pius XI's writings the consequences of the uneasiness of Leo's synthesis of innovative and traditional conceptions of social organization began to emerge. The concept of social justice introduced a positive evaluation of institutional change into the effort to specify the claims of human dignity. The person remains primary. But Piux XI recognized that the social and institutional relationships between persons are not simply rigid containers for transcendental worth. They are living processes in and through which persons in mutual interaction realize and actualize their transcendental dignity. Pius XI's appeal for the *development* of societal institutions which protect dignity in accord with the norm of social justice introduced a new, more dynamic notion of the conditions of dignity into the tradition. The social forms necessary for the protection of human worth are no longer seen as pre-established. Pius XI's tendency to a corporativist social philosophy kept the stable hierarchical model partially alive, but his writings represent an important introduction of active participation and mutuality as defining characteristics of a society built on respect for human dignity. The institutional structures of society are not taken for granted, but must be developed in such a way that basic rights are protected. This shift was an important breakthrough. It began a process by which the institutional order came to be thought of as flexible and subject to change.

In Pius XII the extrinsic, static relation between personal dignity and the institutional forms which protect it almost entirely vanished. Family, property and the state have become structures through which a community of mutually responsible persons organizes itself. Pius XII's frequent discussions of the intrinsic relation of order and morality is evidence of this development. In

John XXIII's treatment of social complexification and Vatican II's stress on historicity and socialization, this active relation between personal freedom, social interaction and institutional structure is present in fully developed form. Paul VI's treatment of integral development and the 1971 Synod's discussion of participation and the right to development are the beginning of a new phase of the tradition—a phase which presumes that personal freedom is simultaneously both inescapably social and intrinsically dependent on developing social structures. Social patterns and institutionalized relationships are themselves seen as structures of the human personality. In these most recent documents we find the viewpoint that human dignity and freedom are conditioned by physical and biological needs, realized in social interaction and association, and structured by the historically changing pattern of the national and international institutions. Human dignity is neither a disembodied spirit separated from the forces of physical and biological process, nor a private inner ghost independent of human interaction, nor a timeless reality beyond political, economic and cultural history.

The tradition has thus arrived at an affirmation of all the civil, political, social, economic and cultural rights set forward in *Pacem in Terris*. It has also concluded that these rights are intrinsically interrelated to each other by interlocking social structures and that their content develops as patterns of social organization change. These most recent developments, therefore, provide a framework capable of incorporating the contributions of both the liberal democratic and Marxist traditions.

During the period we have been examining, therefore, a twofold process of differentiation of the conditions of human dignity has been underway. First, the theory has identified a number of characteristic needs, freedoms and kinds of relationship which must be met or protected in the life of every individual person. For example, human beings depend on food, shelter, and minimum conditions for the preservation of their bodily life. Similarly, the freedom to associate, to participate in political life and to seek and express religious beliefs are also fundamental conditions of this dignity. The existence of every person is dependent on and structured by the associations and relations which he or she forms or is driven into. The ways persons use their physical and intellectual energy and creativity in work form the kinds of persons they become. The same is true of the way they participate in the cultural life of society, their family relationships, their religious beliefs, the kinds of bonds they establish with others through different forms of communication, and the choices they make about where to live. This description of the different "sectors" of individual existence is not exhaustive nor are its domains meant to be mutually exclusive. It is on such a differentiation of the different sectors or domains of human personality, however, that the tradition has based one component of its theory of rights. To each of these essential areas of human existence corresponds a set of human rights which defend human dignity within that sector.

Thus there are rights which protect the dignity of human existence in its bodiliness: the rights to life, bodily integrity, food, clothing, shelter and some minimum degree of health care. There are rights which defend the dignity of the person in work, such as the rights to work, to free initiative in the economic field, to adequate working conditions and to a just wage. Rights such as the right to assembly and association defend individual dignity in its social interactions. This sectoral differentiation of human needs, freedoms and relationships has been at the root of the tradition's attempt to specify the demands of dignity in terms of identifiable human rights.

Secondly, however, rights can be differentiated according to the way their content is mediated by society and social institutions. There are certain fundamental characteristics which belong to the person as such. Life, bodiliness, self-determination, sociability, the need and ability to work, sexuality, family life, and some form of ultimate religious or philosophical convictions are all characteristics of every truly human person. These characteristic aspects of the person, however, can be actualized in different ways in different societies and cultures. They can also be institutionalized in a variety of ways. To say this is not to say that they are entirely socially relative, for they must be realized and institutionalized in social life in some way. To these basic needs, freedoms and forms of relationship which characterize the person and which must be protected if human dignity is to be protected we can give the name "personal rights." The necessity of providing for the realization of these personal rights in societal interaction and communal life gives rise to another kind of right—social rights. These social rights are *conditions* for the preservation of the well-being of the person. They are, however, more than negative boundaries which establish limits which must not be transgressed by society. Human dignity is realized in a positive way through mutuality and social unity. Social rights, then, are expressions of the forms of human interdependence which are indispensable for the realization of human dignity. They specify positive obligations of society toward all its members. For example, the preservation of the personal right to life and health is a value which involves not only the person whose life and health are at stake, but his or her family. It also involves the other members of the society to which he or she belongs. It makes a social claim, a claim about how the individual and the community are interrelated. Because interdependence is an essential aspect of human existence, the preservation of human dignity is a social task. Personal dignity is an attribute of the individual, but it is also mediated socially. The ways persons relate to each other in society either impede or enhance their mutual dignity. This insight is crystallized in the affirmation of a number of social rights by the tradition, such as the rights to medical care, political participation, assembly and association, adequate working conditions, and others. These rights are the social mediation of personal rights.

In addition to these personal and social rights there is a third type of right which can be distinguished according to the kind of social interaction involved in its definition and protection. The primary concern of social rights is the preservation of human dignity in social interdependence. This social existence, however, is shaped and structured by large-scale institutions such as the state, the law, the economy, the health care system, etc. The way these large-scale institutions are organized has indirect but extremely important influence on the possibility of claiming one's personal and social rights. Personal dignity is mediated not only by the realities of social interdependence but also by the way these realities are institutionalized. Thus the tradition has come to affirm a number of conditions which must be present in these macro-institutions if human dignity is to be preserved. These conditions can be called instrumental rights. They include such rights as the right to juridical protection of one's social and personal rights, the right to organize politically and economically, the right to some organized system of social security, and the right to the social, cultural and moral conditions necessary for family life. These two ways of distinguishing rights—according to sectors or dimensions of the human personality and according to the kinds of personal, social or instrumental relationships involved—are helpful keys for unlocking the inner logic of the Roman Catholic rights theory. Employing both perspectives simultaneously, Figure 1 provides a schematic interpretation of the relationships between the rights affirmed by *Pacem in Terris.*

Several important points should be noted concerning this interpretative schema. Catholic rights theory is far removed from individualist or libertarian social philosophy. The theory presented in the encyclicals is personalist, not individualist, and it recognizes that persons are essentially social and institution building beings. Because of this fact the personal rights which belong to every human being in an unmediated way create duties which bind other persons, society and the state. These duties are not simply interpersonal bonds such as those which exist within families and other primary groups. They are also social and political. Consequently the recognition of the full richness of human dignity creates a demand in the human community that the social and instrumental rights in the two outer circles of the diagram be recognized through the appropriate structures.

The advantage of distinguishing the three levels of rights, however, is its acknowledgment of the differing degrees of historical contingency and variability which govern the three types of rights. While the core personal rights have been consistently defended in the tradition's documents, there have been major shifts in its understanding of the appropriate form for instrumental rights. The Roman Catholic tradition thus recognizes that rights have a history, for personal existence in society is itself historical and developing. This historicity is especially evident in the area of social rights, and even more so in the domain of

PERSONAL, SOCIAL AND INSTRUMENTAL RIGHTS: AN INTERPRETATION OF *PACEM IN TERRIS*.

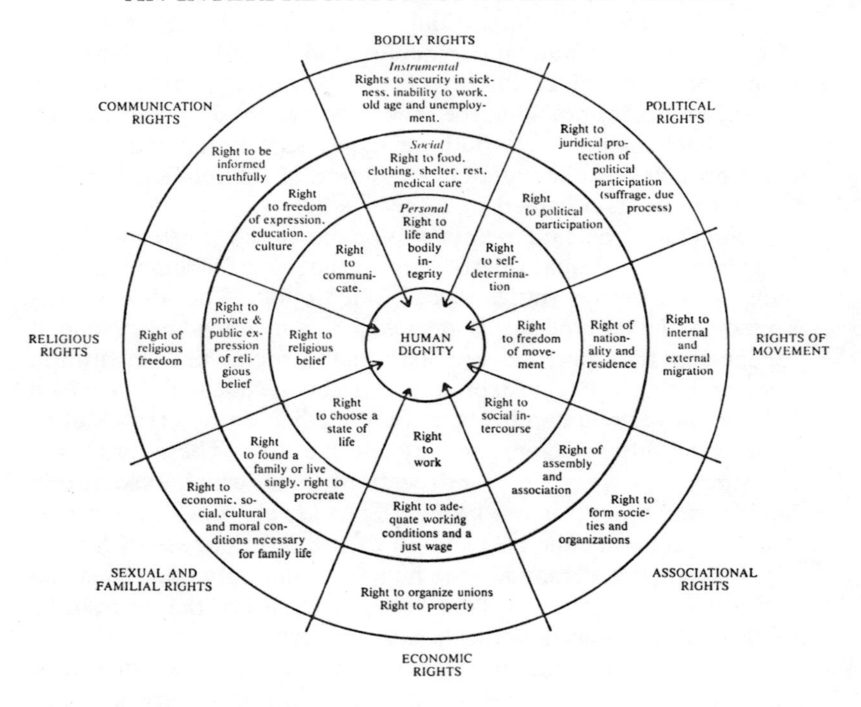

ECONOMIC RIGHTS

Figure 1: Adapted from the Yale Task Force on Population Ethics (D. Christiansen, R. Garet, D. Hollenbach and C. Powers), "Moral Claims, Human Rights and Population Policies," *Theological Studies* 35 (1974), p. 102 (with permission).

instrumental rights. Furthermore, this history has a direction. The social and institutional configurations of human existence are increasingly important in attempts to preserve human dignity. Vatican II has named this historical movement "socialization."

It is also important to note that a particular social right provides the social context for an interrelated group of personal rights, and that particular instrumental rights support clusters of both personal and social rights. Thus the geometrical simplicity of the schema can be deceptive despite its usefulness. There can be no mechanical or mathematically perfect schematization of rights and their relationship. The realization of human dignity is possible only through a constant struggle to achieve a form of integrity which keeps many factors in a living unity with each other, a struggle for "integral development." Thus just as the instrumental right to form labor unions protects and embodies not only the core right to work but other core rights such as the right to self-determination and the right to social intercourse, so instrumental rights concerning family life are necessary for the realization of such personal and social rights as those to food, shelter, political participation, adequate working conditions as well as the rights to found a family and to procreate.

The introduction of the right to development in the Synod document *Justice in the World* ("a dynamic interpenetration of all those fundamental human rights upon which the aspirations of individuals and nations are based") is the most explicit acknowledgment of the interconnectedness of all these personal, social and instrumental rights. The same interconnectedness is evident in the Synod's insistance that the participation of all persons in the shaping of social and political conditions is a prerequisite for the realization of all other rights. The major breakthrough in the period since Vatican II has been the recognition that the relationship between the different rights affirmed by the tradition is a dynamic one. The links between the exercise of different rights are formed by the patterns of human interdependence in society. We shall argue in Chapter Five that this situation of interdependence should lead the tradition to place primary emphasis on the need to protect social rights as it develops in the future.

The right to development affirms that both personal activity and institutional organization must be directed to the creation of a social order in which persons are able to realize their personal rights in mutuality and solidarity with each other.

In the most recent phase of the tradition, the personal rights which have been differentiated since Leo XIII continue to be of central importance. Certain minimum conditions of material existence and of self-determination continue to make moral claims in a complex society. These personal rights are continuously affirmed throughout the tradition and they will continue to be affirmed in the future. Personal rights determine the most basic content of both social and instrumental rights. The post-Conciliar documents give new emphasis, however, to the social and institutional conditions for the realization of these personal rights. The most recent discussions of the right to development and the right to participation place great stress on the need for all persons to be integrated actively into the processes which give direction to society as a whole. The rights to participation and development have become conditions for the realization of all other rights.

The question that this review of the Catholic rights tradition leaves with us is this: Granted the interconnectedness of all these human rights, what are the priority principles for their implementation? Decisions about such priorities are necessary if we are to get from where we are to where we ought to be. The next two chapters will investigate whether the Catholic tradition has anything to contribute to the formation of such practical and strategic decisions about the relative weights to be given various human rights. Chapter Three will briefly examine some of the distinctively Christian grounds for the Catholic rights tradition. It will point out that Christian faith has made an important contribution to the evolution of the theory and can help provide important guidance in the effort to formulate strategic priorities. Chapter Four will further explore the topic by examining how the tradition's theory of justice and love can be used to mediate conflicts of value and establish strategic priorities for the future. Then we will be in a position to evaluate the full worth of the Catholic contribution to the human rights debate and to make some suggestions for its further development.

NOTES

1. Maurice Cranston, "Pope John XXIII on Peace and the Rights of Man," *Political Quarterly* 34 (1963), p. 390.

2. "A Preview of *Mater et Magistra*," in *The Encyclicals and Other Messages of John XXIII*, ed. The Staff of the Pope Speaks Magazine (Washington: TPS Press, 1964), p. 233.

3. *MM*, nos. 219-220. The abbreviations used for official Church documents are indicated in the list of abbreviations on pp. 211–13. The translations quoted are those indicated there, unless otherwise noted.

4. *RN*, no. 7, see *QA*, no. 49.

5. John Courtney Murray, S.J., "Leo XIII: Separation of Church and State," *Theological Studies* 14 (1953), p. 159. See idem, "The Church and Totalitarian Democracy," *Theological Studies* 13, (1952), pp. 525-563. Murray borrowed both the phrase and the notion of "totalitarian democracy" from J. L. Talmon, *The Origins of Totalitarian Democracy* (London: 1952).

6. See Arturo Gaete, "Socialism and Communism: History of a Problem-ridden Condemnation," *LADOC*, September 1973, IV; 1.

7. See Gaete, "Socialism and Communism," p. 12.

8. *Lib*, no. 16. See also *HG*, no. 22; *Diut*, nos. 5, 12 and 23; *QAM*, no. 2; *ID*, nos. 2, 3, 23-26, and *Lib*, nos. 9, 14 and 31.

9. *RN*, no. 40.

10. *RN*, no. 33.

11. See *QAM*, no. 1.

12. Murray, "Leo XIII: Two Concepts of Government," *Theological Studies* 14 (1953), pp. 551-567; idem, "Leo XIII: Two Concepts of Government: II. Government and the Order of Culture," *Theological Studies* 15 (1954), pp. 1-33.

13. *RN*, no. 40.

14. For accounts of this movement in the second half of the nineteenth century, see, for example, Franz H. Mueller, "The Antecedents of *Rerum Novarum*," *Social Justice Review* 44 (1951), pp. 113-116; Lillian Parker Wallace, *Leo XIII and the Rise of Socialism* (Chapel Hill, N.C.; Duke University Press, 1961), chap. XI; Georges Jarlot, S.J., "Les avant-projects de *Rerum Novarum*," *Nouvelle revue théologique* LXXXI (1959), pp. 60-77; idem, *Doctrine pontificale et histoire: L'Enseignment social de Léon XIII, Pie X et Benoît XV vu dans son ambiance historique (1878-1922)* (Rome: Presses de l' Université Grégorienne, 1964), ch. VI.

15. See Wallace, *Leo XIII and Socialism*, p. 267.

16. *RN*, no. 3.

17. *RN*, no. 42. Leo's affirmation of the grave violation of human dignity involved in slavery makes this point in an even more fundamental way. See *Inscrut*, no. 5 and *IP*, esp. nos. 3 and 16.

18. *RN*, no. 2.

19. *RN*, no. 34.

20. *RN*, nos. 43-45; see nos. 20, 32.

21. *RN*, nos. 49-51.

22. *RN*, no. 40.

23. *RN*, no. 37.

24. See Pius X's Apostolic Letter to the French Hierarchy, *Notre charge apostolique, Acta Apostolicae Sedis* 2 (1910), pp. 612-13.

25. See Sandor Agócs, "Christian Democracy and Social Modernism in Italy during the Papacy of Pius X," *Church History* 42 (March, 1973), pp. 73-88; Charles Breunig, "The Condemnation of the *Sillon:* An Episode in the History of Christian Democracy in France," *Church History* 26 (Sept., 1957), pp. 227-44; A. R. Vidler, *A Century of Social Catholicism: 1820-1920* (London: S.P.C.K., 1964), pp. 133-40.

26. The best systematic analysis of Pius XI's social thought is that of Oswald von Nell-Breuning, S.J., *Reorganization of Social Economy: The Social Encyclical Developed and Explained,* trans. Bernard W. Dempsey, S.J. (New York: Bruce, 1939). Nell-Breuning was one of Pius XI's chief advisors on social matters and his hand is evident in both *QA* and *DR*.

27. *QA*, no. 61.

28. *QA*, no. 106.

29. An excellent review of this understanding of needs can be found in Jean-Yves Calvez, S.J. and Jacques Perrin, S.J., *The Church and Social Justice: The Social Teaching of the Popes from Leo XIII to Pius XII (1878-1959),* trans. J. R. Kirwan (Chicago: Henry Regnery Company, 1961), chap. VIII. See Pius XI's *DIM*, no. 4.

30. It is clear that the papal tradition up to John XXIII or perhaps Paul VI's *Octogesima Adveniens* (1971) had an insufficiently differentiated conception of the various forms of Marxism and socialism. See Richard L. Camp, *The Papal Ideology of Social Reform: A Study in Historical Development, 1878-1967* (Leiden: E. J. Brill, 1967), chap. III, "The Errors of Socialism and Communism"; Arturo Gaete, "Socialism and Communism"; idem, "Social Catholicism and Marxism in the 19th Century," *LADOC*, January, 1974, IV, 23. Some of the implications of the recent shift in viewpoint will be pointed out below in the discussion of *Octogesima Adveniens*.

31. See *DR*, nos. 30-31; *QA*, no. 112.

32. *QA*, nos. 116 and 120.

33. See *QA*, no. 119.

34. *DR*, no. 29.

35. *DR*, no. 29.

36. *DR*, no. 10.

37. A sympathetic treatment of these complex issues can be found in Anthony Rhodes, *The Vatican in the Age of the Dictators (1922-1945)*, (New York: Holt, Rinehart and Winston, 1973). See also William M. Harrigan, "Nazi Germany and the Holy See, 1933-1936: The Historical Background of *Mit Brennender Sorge*," *Catholic Historical Review* XLVII (1961-62), pp. 164-98. A much more critical evaluation of the

papal response to these regimes is that of Guenter Lewy, *The Catholic Church and Nazi Germany* (New York: McGraw-Hill, 1965).

38. *NAB,* nos. 49 and 57.

39. *MBS,* no. 12.

40. See, for example, *QA,* nos. 57, 58, 88, 110, 126; *DR* 50-55. The different notions of justice which can be found in the official documents are analyzed in detail in Chapter Four.

41. See *QA,* no. 49.

42. See *QA,* no. 45.

43. *QA,* no. 49.

44. *DR,* no. 27.

45. See Richard L. Camp, *Papal Ideology,* p. 41.

46. The importance of this address for the subsequent development of the tradition is evident from the fact that it was cited eleven times in Pope John's *Pacem in Terris,* the most systematic and influential of the modern papal documents.

47. Christmas Address, 1942, in Vincent A. Yzermans, ed., *The Major Addresses of Pope Pius XII,* 2 vols. (St. Paul: North Central Publishing Company, 1961), vol. II, p. 54.

48. Christmas Address, 1944, in Yzermans, II, p. 82.

49. Christmas Address, 1942, in Yzermans, II, p. 56.

50. "The Church has nothing in common with the narrowness of a sect or with an imperialism tied to its own traditions. She works with every care for the achievement of that end which St. Thomas Aquinas, disciple of Aristotle, assigns to life in community, that is, to hold men together with the bond of friendship." Address of February 20, 1946, in Yzermans, I, p. 81.

51. *SP,* no. 5.

52. Christmas Address, 1941, in Yzermans, II, p. 42. See Christmas Address, 1952, in Yzermans, II, p. 163.

53. Christmas Address, 1951, in Yzermans, II, p. 156.

54. As examples of this negative evaluation of technological developments in European existentialist thought, see Karl Jaspers, *Man in the Modern Age,* trans. Eden and Cedar Paul (Garden City, N.Y.: Doubleday Anchor Books, 1957), esp. Pt. One, and Gabriel Marcel, *Man Against Mass Society,* trans. G. S. Fraser (Chicago: Regnery, 1965), esp. Pt. One, chaps. III and IV.

55. Christmas Address, 1952, in Yzermans, II, p. 163.

56. The most obvious modern counter-position to that of Pius XII is that of Reinhold Niebuhr. See esp. his *An Interpretation of Christian Ethics* (New York: Harper & Brothers, 1935), chap. IV, "The Relevance of an Impossible Ethical Ideal."

57. The phrase is Paul Tillich's. For a development of its meaning as descriptive of the state of mind which imagines a form of human life which is utopian (literally, *ou topos,* no place) and which is unrealizable under the conditions of finite human freedom, see Tillich, *Systematic*

Theology, 3 vols. in 1 (Chicago: University of Chicago Press, 1967) vol. II, pp. 33-36.

58. For an important theological discussion of the relation between human finitude and the unconditional worth of the person that has been influential in recent Roman Catholic theology, see Karl Rahner, S.J., "The Dignity and Freedom of Man," in *Theological Investigations,* 14 vols., trans. Cornelius Ernst, *et al.* (New York: Seabury, 1963), Vol. II, pp. 245-49.

59. See Christmas Address, 1952, and Christmas Address, 1954, in Yzermans, II, pp. 162-163 and 202-204, 222.

60. Christmas Address, 1942, in Yzermans, II, pp. 60-61.

61. Address of December 6, 1953, in Yzermans, I, pp. 270-271.

62. Pentecost Address, 1941, in Yzermans, I, p. 31.

63. *PT,* no. 159.

64. For a lively discussion of the causes and consequences of John XXIII's innovations, see E. E. Y. Hales, *Pope John and His Revolution* (Garden City, N.Y.: Doubleday, 1965).

65. *MM,* no. 46-49.

66. *MM,* no. 59.

67. See the very important section of *Mater et Magistra* on the complexification of social structures, nos. 59-67.

68. *MM,* no. 51.

69. See above, p. 43.

70. See, e.g., *MM,* nos. 157 and 200.

71. An especially helpful discussion of this key aspect of the argument in *Mater et Magistra* can be found in Jean-Yves Calvez, S.J., *The Social Thought of John XXIII: Mater et Magistra,* trans. George J. M. McKenzie, S.M. (Chicago: Regnery, 1964), chap. 1, and idem, "Possibilities of Freedom in Tomorrow's Complex Society," in *Freedom and Man,* ed. John Courtney Murray, S.J. (New York: Kenedy, 1965), pp. 168-182.

72. *MM,* no. 63.

73. *MM,* no. 65. See *DH,* no. 6 and *GS,* no. 26.

74. *MM,* nos. 60, 65 and 66.

75. *PT,* no. 9.

76. *PT,* no. 31.

77. *PT,* no. 34.

78. *PT,* no. 135.

79. *PT,* nos. 70 and 71.

80. All these rights are listed in *PT,* nos. 11-27.

81. *PT,* no. 155.

82. Karl Rahner, a theologian whose influence was strongly felt during the drafting of *Gaudium et Spes,* has stated the issue clearly: our knowledge of the historically concrete specifications of human dignity "is itself a historically becoming process" and "essentially unfinished." Even more radically, it is not simply our knowledge of these concrete

specifications of dignity which are historical, but the ontologically determinate conditions for the realization of dignity are themselves at least in part historical. Human dignity is penetrated to its core by historicity. In Rahner's words, "There is no zone of the person which is absolutely inaccessible to such influences from without." "The Dignity and Freedom of Man," pp. 237 and 242.

83. *GS,* no. 3.

84. See *GS,* no. 5.

85. *GS,* no. 10.

86. Reinhold Niebuhr has given the most powerful modern treatment of this tendency of the human spirit and its ethical consequences in his *The Nature and Destiny of Man,* 2 vols. (New York: Charles Scribners' Sons, 1964), vol. 1, chaps. VII and VIII.

87. *GS,* no. 13.

88. See *GS,* nos. 14, 23, 25.

89. *GS,* no. 25.

90. *GS,* no. 25.

91. *GS,* nos. 63 and 65.

92. See *GS,* nos. 14-16.

93. In Murray's running commentary on *DH* in the Abbott-Gallagher edition of the Council documents, p. 687, note 22.

94. Pietro Pavan, "Declaration on Religious Freedom," in Herbert Vorgrimler, ed., *Commentary on the Documents of Vatican II,* 5 vols. (New York: Herder and Herder, 1969), vol. IV, pp. 76-78.

95. *DH,* no. 1.

96. In Murray's commentary in the Abbott-Gallagher edition of the Council documents, p. 677, note 4.

97. See the important no. 7 of *DH* in this regard.

98. Andrew Greeley, *No Bigger Than Necessary. An Alternative to Socialism, Capitalism and Anarchism* (New York: Meridian, 1977), p. 12. Greeley remarks that "No one, as far as I am aware, has noted the massive shift of emphasis between *Quadragesimo Anno* and *Pacem in Terris,* on the one hand, and *Populorum Progressio* on the other." It would be more accurate to state that few would regard the shift as negatively as Greeley does. For example, Quentin Lauer sees it as nothing less than an "epoch making" development in Catholic social thought. (Roger Garaudy and Quentin Lauer, S.J., *A Christian-Communist Dialogue,* New York: Doubleday, 1968, p. 158). Jean-Marie Aubert states that its publication "a marqué une date primordiale dans ce progres doctrinal." (*Pour une théologie de l' âge industriel,* vol. 1er, Paris: Cerf, 1971, p. 145.)

99. *PP,* no. 14.

100. *PP,* no. 20.

101. *PP,* no. 6.

102. *PP,* no. 16, see nos. 28 and 34.

103. Garaudy and Lauer, *Christian-Communist Dialogue,* p. 156.

104. *PP,* no. 6.

105. *PP,* no. 9. The citation is from *Gaudium et Spes,* no. 63.

106. *PP,* no. 43.

107. *PP,* no. 21.

108. Here the papal approach can be contrasted once again with that of Reinhold Niebuhr. For Niebuhr the fact of conflict between aspects of the total good of persons and society implies that all moral decisions are in some sense compromised. Niebuhr's position is a complex one. See the excellent analysis in Gene Outka, *Agape: An Ethical Analysis* (New Haven: Yale University Press, 1972), pp. 24-34; 78-81. In the main, however, Niebuhr would regard all actions which fall short of establishing a state of frictionless harmony between interests and goods as somehow morally imperfect. Since this is the necessary condition of human beings in history, persons always live in a compromised state. The position of the Roman Catholic tradition represented by *Populorum Progressio* acknowledges this kind of imperfection. It would claim, though, that this does not mean that *moral* compromise is involved. Moral integrity within a person or a society is not to be identified with the attainment of an unhistorical state beyond conflict. It is rather the achievement of mutual respect within the limits and conditions of history. To live in conflicted history is not a compromise but the way in which human beings attain their human perfection. Human perfection is not divine perfection and should not be faulted because it is not. On this issue see Bruno Schüller, "Zur Rede von der radicalen sittlichen Forderung," *Theologie und Philosophie* 46 (1971), pp. 321-341 and Peter Knauer, S.J., "The Hermeneutic Function of the Principle of Double Effect," *Natural Law Forum* 12 (1967), pp. 132-162, esp. section VI.

109. *OA*, nos. 32-35.

110. *OA*, no. 40.

111. See *OA*, nos. 43, 46 and 47.

112. John Courtney Murray has stated that the much more systematic lists of principles and rights in *Pacem in Terris* similarly function as norms of discernment. See his "Key Themes in the Encyclical," appended to the America Press edition of *PT* (New York, 1963), p. 57.

113. *JW,* no. 15.

114. *JW,* no. 12.

115. *JW,* no. 10.

116. *JW,* no. 9.

117. *JW,* no. 16.

118. *JW,* no. 18.

119. *JW,* nos. 17, 18, 19, 23, 24, 25, 26.

120. *JW,* nos. 41-48.

121. Speaking of the total corpus of Roman Catholic "social doctrine" Calvez and Perrin state that "the teaching set forth by the Church under this heading is not a theoretical construction made independently of the circumstances which have given rise to it, but the historical response to an historical problem." *The Church and Social Justice,* p. 5.

Chapter Three
A Christian Theory of Rights?

In tracing and analyzing the historical development of the theory of rights we have so far been only minimally concerned with the religious significance of human dignity and human rights. This religious dimension is the direct concern of this chapter. Roman Catholic social ethics understands the human person as a being whose significance and worth are deeply rooted in a relationship with God. The way the tradition interprets this relationship with God has played an important role in the formation and development of the theory of rights. This chapter will attempt to make such influence explicit.

There are two reasons why explicitly religious statements about human dignity are important in analyzing the Roman Catholic contribution to the human rights debate.

First, the usefulness of the Catholic human rights tradition in a pluralist society is partially dependent on the degree to which its conclusions are persuasive to those who do not share the Christian faith. Its usefulness in the broader ecumenical Christian community is also partially determined by the theological perspective which it presupposes. Both the pluralist-secular and the ecumenical-Christian contexts raise the question of the relation between universalist moral claims and particularist religious beliefs for the Catholic rights tradition in an urgent way. The two parts of this chapter will examine how Christian faith has been involved in shaping the notion of human dignity and human rights in the pre- and post-Conciliar periods.

The second reason for exploring these theological foundations is more practical and oriented to concrete policy questions. The way any human right is socially limited depends on the way human interrelationships are understood. As we have seen in analyzing the liberal democratic and Marxist theories, the model of human community one adopts is largely determinant of the rights which are given priority in social policy. Similarly, the differentiation of personal, social and instrumental rights which was traced in the conclusion of the previous chapter reveals why the understanding of the nature of human community and the function of social institutions is centrally important in Catholic thinking about the implementation of rights. When the Catholic tradition discusses the nature of human community, it consistently speaks of love as a bond which unites persons in society. The meaning of love in any Christian ethic is profoundly dependent on the way that ethic appeals to both religious symbols and theological doctrines. God's love for the world and the love exemplified and realized in Jesus Christ are important elements in the conception of human love which is ethically normative for Christians.

Consequently, the discussion of the priorities among human rights would be incomplete without attention to the way the religious symbols and theological doctrines of Christian faith enter the Roman Catholic social ethic. This chapter will analyze the theological foundations of the Catholic rights theory with both of these concerns in view. The practical and strategic implications of this analysis will be developed in Chapter Five.

THE NATURE OF THE HUMAN PERSON

The central theological affirmation at the foundation of the Roman Catholic rights theory is that the human person is a living image of God. The doctrine of the *imago Dei* runs through all the major documents we have been examining.[1] *Pacem in Terris* begins its synthetic recapitulation of the tradition by recalling the doctrine's biblical foundation: "God also created man in His own image and likeness" (Gen. 1:26), "endowed him with intelligence and freedom, and made him lord of creation." [2] By virtue of this fact, the encyclical goes on, every human person "has rights and duties of his own, flowing directly and simultaneously from his very nature. These rights are therefore universal, inviolable, and inalienable." [3] A similar theme occupies a central place in the Second Vatican Council's discussion of the theological basis of human dignity. The words of *Gaudium et Spes* are worth reproducing at length:

> According to the almost unanimous opinion of believers and unbelievers alike, all things on earth should be related to man as their center and crown.
>
> But what is man? About himself he has expressed, and continues to express, many divergent and even contradictory opinions. In these he often exalts himself as the absolute measure of all things or debases himself to the point of despair. The result is doubt and anxiety.
>
> The Church understands these problems. Endowed with light from God, she can offer solutions to them so that man's true situation can be portrayed and his defects explained, while at the same time his dignity and destiny are justly acknowledged.
>
> For sacred Scripture teaches that man was created "to the image of God," is capable of knowing and loving his creator, and was appointed by Him as master of all earthly creatures that he might subdue them and use them to God's glory.[4]

These passages from *Pacem in Terris* and *Gaudium et Spes* point up a basic tension running through the Catholic tradition. One pole of the tension is represented by the style of theological thought found in *Pacem in Terris,* which closely identifies the *imago Dei* with the fact that human beings are endowed with intelligence and freedom. This is the style of neo-scholastic theology and philosophy. Its approach provides theological justification for appeals to reason and natural law as the bases of a theory of human rights. The other pole, represented by *Gaudium et Spes,* places greater emphasis on the contribution which Christian faith can make to the theory of rights in a pluralistic world. Christians are "endowed with light from God" which makes clearer both the reality of human dignity and its concrete demands.

The presence of these two poles shows that the relation of the Catholic tradition to secular philosophical reflection on human rights on the one hand and to the more biblical style of ethical thought found in Protestantism on the other is not a simple relationship. The pole which emphasizes reason and natural law in developing the theory of rights is viewed differently by secular philosophers and Protestant theologians. For example, in commenting on *Pacem in Terris,* the political philosopher Maurice Cranston praised John XXIII's appeal to natural law as the foundation of his human rights charter. In Cranston's view the encyclical is important precisely because it is

> apparent that Pope John does not look on natural law in the orthodox Catholic way as something needing clerical interpretation, and limited by the exigencies of the Church's mission. Pope John's concept of natural law is something closer to that of the stoic tradition: it is something discernible by the eye of reason alone, and something which pertains to humanity as a whole.[5]

It is precisely the encyclical's confidence that freedom and intelligence are images of the divine in human beings that enables *Pacem in Terris* to address its discussion of rights not only to Christians but to all persons of good will.[6]

This same confidence, however, is the object of Protestant theological criticism. From the viewpoint of many Protestants such an interpretation of the ethical implications of the *imago Dei* fails to recognize the depth of human brokenness, sin and the need for redemption. Reason alone is incapable of discovering the actual demands of human dignity. Without the aid of grace, human freedom is incapable of fully responding to these demands. Even so humanistic a Protestant thinker as Paul Tillich charged *Pacem in Terris* with excessive optimism in this regard. Speaking as both a Protestant theologian and an existentialist philosopher Tillich put his objection this way:

> I see human nature determined by the conflict between the goodness of man's essential being and the ambiguity of his

> actual being, his life, under the conditions of existence. The goodness of his essential nature gives him his greatness, his dignity, the demand, embodied in him, to be acknowledged as a person. On the other hand, the predicament in which he finds himself, the estrangement from his true being, drives him into the opposite direction, preventing him from fulfilling in actual life what he essentially is. It makes all his doings, and all that which is done by him, ambiguous, bad, as well as good. And one should not appeal to "all men of good will" as the encyclical does. One should appeal to all men knowing that in the best will there is an element of bad will and that in the worst there will be an element of good will.[7]

Thus for Tillich and other Protestant thinkers an adequate social ethic must take the conflicts and blindnesses characteristic of fallen humanity more seriously than *Pacem in Terris* and the natural law ethic does.

Protestant thinkers have also criticized this ethic for granting human nature a false independence in the face of God's sovereign claim on the freedom of human beings. In the words of a statement prepared at the Theological Consultation on Human Rights of the World Alliance of Reformed Churches:

> We understand the basic theological contribution of the Christian faith, in these matters, to be the grounding of fundamental human rights in God's right to, that is, his claim on human beings. This is to say that human rights are ultimately grounded not in human nature; nor are they conditioned by individual or collective human achievements in history. They reflect the covenant of God's faithfulness to his people and the glory of his love for the church and the world.[8]

Both of these distinctively Protestant theological emphases on the doctrine of sin and on the sovereignty of God have led to an ethic which grants greater weight to both social conflicts and to social duties than Catholic thought has traditionally done. The differences are not simply theoretical. They affect interpretations of what is practically possible in the human rights field and influence the determination of strategic priorities in the effort to implement human rights.

The second pole of the tension between universalist and particularist warrants for human rights theory—that represented by *Gaudium et Spes'* belief that the Christian faith provides privileged insight into the demands of human dignity—is also variously received by secular philosophers and Protestant theologians. Political philosopher Leo Strauss, for example, suggests that efforts to found a theory of rights on religious belief flies in the face of the entire project of secular political thought since John Locke. The modern project is based on the conviction that "natural law or natural right should be kept independent of theology and its controversies."[9] Similarly, Frederick Olafson argues that such independence from theology is a practical necessity if any degree of social harmony is to be achieved. In Olafson's view, "A pluralistic society that tries to make its unifying political and moral principles religious in any nontrivial sense is in for trouble."[10] Theologian Jürgen Moltmann, on the other hand, maintains that if the Christian community is to be true to itself it must seek to understand human rights theologically. In his words:

> On the ground of the creation of man and woman in the image of God, on the ground of the incarnation of God for the reconciliation of the world, and on the ground of the coming of the kingdom of God as the consummation of history, the concern entrusted to Christian theology is one for the humanity of persons as well as for their ongoing rights and duties. The specific task of Christian theology in these matters is grounding fundamental human rights on God's right to—i.e., his claim on—human beings, their human dignity, their fellowship, their rule over the earth, and their future.[11]

Thus, in the manner of *Gaudium et Spes,* Moltmann develops his Christian interpretation of human dignity by appealing to the central beliefs and doctrines of Christianity.

These diverse responses to the tension inherent in the way the Catholic tradition has appealed to philosophical and theological interpretations of human dignity and rights raise questions about both the coherence and usefulness of the tradition itself. In fact, however, there has been a major development in the theological aspects of the Catholic rights tradition since the Second Vatican Council which clarifies the relation between the Roman Catholic rights theory and the analyses of both secular philosophers and Protestant theologians. In order to understand this development, it will be helpful to sketch its point of departure in neo-scholastic thought.

From Leo XIII to John XXIII the theological affirmation that persons are created in the image of God was used to support a very great confidence in the power of the human mind to know the most fundamental structures of human existence. As images of God, human beings share in the wisdom and knowledge of God. Therefore, universal moral principles and basic human rights are knowable by human reasoning and analysis. This reasoning is capable of reaching very general conclusions about the moral life, such as the fundamental norm of human dignity and the governance of all things by the mind and will of God. It is capable of seeing that human persons are essentially both free and interdependent. They are dependent on minimum levels of food, clothing, and shelter. Reason can discover the values of work as an expression of human creativity, the importance of the family as the primary environment for the nurtùrance of human worth, the necessity of government, the need for a division of labor, and the binding character of contracts.[12] The human rights which are listed in various places throughout the documents up to Vatican II are derived from reasoned reflection on these various dimensions of social and individual life and from an attempt to discover the relation between these dimensions and the dignity of the person. In these pre-Conciliar documents, therefore, the theory of rights rests on human reason and should be accessible to all reasonable people.

Such claims for the power of reason are coherent with the theological doctrines which underlie the ethical vision of the tradition. They represent one aspect of the total theological vision, namely, that which sees human rationality as a reflection of and participation in the wisdom of God. For all their defense of the role of reason in the formation of the theory of rights, however, it is clear that the documents of the pre-Vatican II period never affirmed that any of their "reasonings" were independent of the influence of Christian doctrine. Indeed, precisely the opposite was the case. One phrase occurs frequently in the descriptions of the epistemological justifications which are given for various ethical claims: reason enlightened by revelation.[13] The coherence of Christian doctrine with the conclusions of "right reason" is one of the basic methodological principles of the theology of these documents. This coherence functions as a negative norm in the development of the ethic. Its negative function is based on the supposition that reason itself cannot contradict any of the ethical implications of fundamental Christian doctrine.[14] Doctrine also helps to fill out the shape of the structure of human dignity in a positive way. In affirming that persons are children of the same common Father, redeemed by Christ, called to a destiny beyond the world, and truly free only in response to grace, Christian faith claims to reveal other dimensions of personhood than those derived from seeing humanity as defined by the capacity for rational thought. These various dimensions of the human person are all integrally related to each other. Thus Christian doctrines can provide positive guidance for understanding the role and use of reason in relation to other, transrational dimensions of the person. In the words of Leo XIII:

> Those, therefore, who to the study of philosophy unite obedience to the Christian faith, are philosophizing in the best possible way, for the splendor of the divine truths, received into the mind, helps the understanding and not only detracts in no wise from its dignity, but adds greatly to its nobility, keenness and stability.[15]

Several characteristics of the interrelation of faith and reason become clear from an examination of how ethical judgments are actually made and defended in the pre-Conciliar documents. First, it is evident that the neo-scholastic approach to the nature of the human person and his or her rights does not use reason in a simply apologetic or defensive way. Its appeals to philosophical anthropology, to social and legal philosophy and to analytic social thought are not simply "rationalizations" of ethical conclusions held on strictly religious grounds. These nontheological modes of analysis are genuinely constitutive of the structure of the rights theory of the modern Roman Catholic tradition. For example, the conclusions concerning the existence of a right to a living wage are formed by quite specific philosophic notions of the relation between human freedom and material needs and, especially in Pius XI, by economic analysis of the relationship between wages, unemployment and profits. These "reasoned" analyses make a contribution both to the developing theory of rights in the tradition and to the discovery of what rights actually exist. This contribution is properly their own, and the rights theory could not exist without it. This contribution, however, is not autonomously separated from the theology which also helps to shape the rights theory.

The way in which this theological influence is operative throughout the discussion of rights is as a perspective which informs, limits and guides all the deliberation and discussion concerning the full richness of the dignity of the person and his or her rights. The most basic influence on the Christian believer's standpoint toward the human world is his or her understanding of the nature of ultimate reality—the nature of God.[16] How one is oriented toward this ultimate reality will shape all other perceptions and understandings of human existence and interrelationship. For example, the Lordship of God over the human race is seen as a rule of justice and love. The Christian's vision of the way society should be ordered is formed by this vision of the nature of God.[17] From an examination of the biblical record, in fact, *Rerum Novarum* concluded that "God Himself seems to incline rather to those who suffer misfortune; for Jesus Christ calls the poor 'blessed'; He lovingly invites those in labor and grief to come to Him for solace; and He displays the tenderest charity toward the lowly and the oppressed." [18] The Christian notion of the redemptive activity of God in the world also shapes the perceived content of moral obligation in society. God's redeeming activity is a model of Christian action—action which should lead to the increase of genuine freedom among persons in history. The call which comes to all persons from God is further specified by the doctrine of the incarnation. In the act of assuming humanity to himself in Christ, God is visible as a model of what the human response to the world should be. The Christology which sees in Jesus the incarnation of the Divine Logos through which the universe was created has direct influence on the moral perspective of Christians.[19] This theological model shapes the Christian moral task as one which seeks to realize the full potentiality of creation in the union of persons in society, and, ultimately, in union with God through Christ.

Thus doctrines of God as Creator and Lord, as Redeemer and as incarnate in Jesus Christ all picture the ultimate ground of human existence as a Person who is just, who is loving, especially toward the poor and oppressed, who seeks the freedom and liberation of all, and who is the source and substance of the unity and order of the universe. Christians are called to image forth this God in their individual and social lives. They are called "to be perfect as their heavenly Father is perfect" (Mt. 5:48).

The relation between reason and revelation in the pre-Vatican II ethic is the relation of differentiated, analytical thinking about the dignity of the person and about the concrete relationships between persons on the one hand and the standpoint from which this thinking proceeds on the other. The Christian standpoint or perspective provides motivation for moral behavior and shapes the attitudes which are characteristic of the Christian moral agent. Within this perspective, dimensions of the person and of social life are brought into high relief and are shown to be definitive of human dignity and, thus, of moral obligation. The non-instrumental value of the person, the centrality of freedom, the importance of building all order and unity in society on a communion of persons rather than on the suppression or subordination of the person to the group, the special claims of the poor and the oppressed, the goodness of the material conditions such as the body, food, shelter, work, property, the family and the state—all these central affirmations of the Roman Catholic rights theory are brought into the foreground by the doctrinal and symbolic background of Christian faith.

It is this relationship between reason and revelation which explains the fact that the neo-scholastic tradition simultaneously maintained that Christian faith makes a radically important contribution to the moral existence of persons in society,[20] and that the basic claims presented in the tradition can be known without explicit adherence to this faith.[21] The relation of religious doctrines and symbols to the claims formulated as rights and duties does not have the form of a deductive logic. The documents do not start with a theological doctrine or religious symbol and then, by a form of strictly syllogistic reasoning, conclude to a particular kind of concrete moral obligation.[22] The connection between rights and duties on the one hand and doctrines and symbols on the other derives from the power which these latter have to evoke a coherent and living vision of the relation between persons in society, a vision of the structure of human dignity.[23] The reality of human dignity is a theological reality. Every human person *is* in fact an image of God, created in and redeemed by Christ, called to the kingdom of God, etc. The reality of human dignity and its structure do not depend for their existence upon the knowledge or recognition of human agents. However, precisely as images of God, human persons do in fact have the ability to know and respect the dimensions of human dignity in at least an imperfect way.

Thus the presupposition of the neo-scholastic theory is that it is possible to formulate a unified and adequate vision of the person through the use of philosophical, empirical and social reason and that this vision corresponds with the perspectives supplied by faith and theology. Also, the concrete and specific moral demands which arise from this vision are themselves necessarily discovered by reason. What the neo-scholastic tradition does not suppose, however, is that such reasoned understanding of the person and concrete conclusions about social obligation may always be incomplete, partial and even ambiguous. The "fit" between reason and revelation, nature and grace or natural law ethics and Christian ethics is seen as a tight and stable one. The relation between the two sides of this relationship is a relation of harmony and reinforcement. In the words of Pius XII, "The Church does not say that morality belongs purely, in the sense of exclusively, to her; but that it belongs wholly to her." [24]

This understanding has important consequences for the

theory of rights. The conviction of the harmony between faith and reason is part of a more generalized conviction that harmony and unity are more fundamental characteristics of the world than are conflict and diversity. In emphasizing the congruity between the Christian perspectives on human rights and the conclusions one should expect to be forthcoming from "men of good will," actual conflicts in the human rights debates are methodologically minimized. The vision of the person in society which neo-scholasticism affirms implies that the apparent conflicts between rights are reconcilable by a rational theory of justice which is knowable by all. The unity of persons in society is thus a unity within the organically structured relations described by these norms of justice. Justice provides the framework of social unity, and love brings this framework to life. Justice and love, therefore, are related as matter and form or as body and soul—with this relationship understood in a thoroughly integrated way.[25] The emphasis throughout is on organic unity, complementarity and reconciliation, rather than on conflict. As we shall see in the next section, however, there is another way to conceive the relations between justice and love, harmony and conflict, faith and reason. If the meaning of justice is always somewhat ambiguous and incomplete because of the conditioned and imperfect nature of social and philosophical analysis, then Christian faith and love assume a different role in social ethics. They are not simply the life and soul of a reasonable and harmonious social order, but sources for the discovery and creation of an order which protects human dignity concretely. They become ways of relating to other persons and the world which continually modify, challenge, heal, transform and perfect justice. It is such an understanding of the faith/reason and love/justice relationships which characterizes the Conciliar and post-Conciliar ethic to which we now turn.

FROM FAITH AND REASON TO CHRISTIANITY AND CULTURE

A major development in the tradition's theological understanding of human rights took place at the Second Vatican Council. The changes in official Roman Catholic theology which occurred at the Council were radical and their effects have been evident in the major social documents which have been issued since the Council. The Council struck out in new directions in both theology and philosophy. It continued, however, to employ many of the central methodological approaches and substantive conclusions characteristic of the pre-Conciliar period.

Let us begin our examination where *Gaudium et Spes* begins. The treatment of "the signs of the times" in the "Introductory Statement" of the Constitution states that the present time is one of "true social and cultural transformation."[26] Though in its conclusions *Gaudium et Spes* is rightly regarded as an optimistic document, like Tillich and the Protestant tradition it sees very powerful evidence for human brokenness in contemporary culture. One of the primary causes of grief and anxiety in modern social life is a breakdown of basic patterns of meaning, a loss of coherence between the diverse forms of knowledge and technique which humanity has developed, and an increasing inability to conduct genuinely communicative social and political discourse. In the words of the Council:

> Although the world of today has a very vivid sense of its unity and how one man depends on another in needful solidarity, it is most greviously torn into opposing camps by conflicting forces. For political, social, economic, racial, and ideological disputes still continue bitterly, and with them the peril of a war which would reduce everything to ashes. True, there is growing exchange of ideas, but the very words by which key concepts are expressed take on quite different meanings in diverse ideological systems.[27]

In other words, increasing consciousness of the divisions between nations, classes, races and ideological groups has had a corrosive effect on the unity of human self-understanding.

This diversification or increasing pluralism in human self-understanding is attributed to several causes by the Conciliar and post-Conciliar documents. First, technological and scientific advancement has been lopsided, both within nation-states and internationally. Consequently, economic, social and political inequality has been exacerbated by the very tools which hold the potential for enhancing human solidarity and personal dignity. *Gaudium et Spes* describes this increased inequality both as a social fact and as a moral failure:

> While an enormous mass of people still lack the absolute necessities of life, some, even in less advanced countries, live sumptuously or squander wealth. Luxury and misery rub shoulders. While the very few enjoy very great freedom of choice the many are deprived of almost all possibility of acting on their own initiative and responsibility, and often subsist in living and working conditions unworthy of human beings.[28]

Populorum Progressio predicts that the present forms of economic organization and regulation will lead to a deepening of the divide which separates economic classes and to increased social conflict.[29] The Synod document on *Justice in the World* affirms that:

> Unless combatted and overcome by social and political action, the influence of the new industrial and technological order favors the concentration of wealth, power and decision-making in the hands of a small or private controlling group.[30]

The neo-scholastic vision of a harmonious society has undergone a significant revision in these passages.

A pluralism in self-understandings and the resulting potential for conflict in the world are also traced to the growth of scientific and technological specialization. It is true that such specialization can lead to deepening humanity's knowledge of its own dignity and of the structures which promote this dignity. *Gaudium et Spes* and subsequent documents affirm and welcome this aspect of the process of modernization.[31] Both the hard and soft sciences are differentiated approaches to knowledge of the world and of human existence. They provide indispensable knowledge of the conditions necessary for the protection of human dignity.

They can, however, easily become forces leading to deepened division within society. They can be used to legitimate visions of the nature of the person in society which are partial and exclusive of dimensions of the human reality which are beyond the reach of their methods. When such an exclusivist use is made of legitimate scientific insight, the potential for conflict which already exists in a situation of social inequality is increased. As Paul VI put it:

> Methodological necessity and ideological presuppositions too often lead the human sciences to isolate, in various situations, certain aspects of man, and yet to give these an explanation which claims to be complete or at least an interpretation which is meant to be all-embracing from a purely quantitative or phenomenological point of view. This scientific reduction betrays a dangerous presumption. To give a privileged position in this way to such an aspect of analysis is to mutilate man and, under the pretext of a scientific procedure, to make it impossible to understand man in his totality.
>
> One must be no less attentive to the action which the human sciences can instigate, giving rise to the elaboration of models of society to be subsequently imposed on men as scientifically tested types of behavior. Man can then become the object of manipulations directing his desires and needs and modifying his behavior and even his system of values. There is no doubt that there exists here a grave danger for the societies of tomorrow and for man himself. For even if all agree to build a new society at the service of man, it is still essential to know what sort of man is in question.[32]

Here, scientific knowledge is regarded as a potential cause of the breakdown of a common language for the interpretation of the fundamental values linked with human dignity and, more practically, as a means which can lead to a diminished form of social life.

This negative note in the analysis of the potential consequences of technological change, scientific advance and social interpretation was not new at the Council. Indeed, this negative note is certainly less pronounced in *Gaudium et Spes* than, for example, in the addresses of Pius XII. What is new in *Gaudium et Spes* and later documents, however, is the radical seriousness with which the challenges of pluralism are viewed. The dangers of loss of common meaning for basic moral terms, of differentiated perception due to social inequality and of incomplete views of the person brought about by methodological specialization are not only dangers which beset those who are intellectually obtuse, morally of "bad will," or religiously unfaithful, as Pius XII sometimes seemed to assume. These dangers have entered into the definition of the problematic of a *Christian* social ethic and theory of human rights.

At Vatican II official Catholicism came to an awareness that modern society is faced with a crisis of moral reason itself. In pointing out the social, economic and methodological conditions which both direct and limit the use of human reflection on moral problems, the tradition has significantly altered the way in which it speaks of the use of reason in the process of moral deliberation and discernment. "Reason" does not have a univocal meaning which is capable of providing univocal answers to the basic moral questions of society. Neither is reason sufficiently stable in its meaning to be used as a simple and well-defined tool for clarifying ethical questions within the Church itself.

Gaudium et Spes states the new problem facing the Roman Catholic tradition in these words:

> In the face of modern development of the world, an ever increasing number of people are raising the most basic questions or recognizing them with a new sharpness: what is man? What is this sense of sorrow, of evil, of death, which continues to exist despite so much progress? What is the purpose of these victories, purchased at so high a cost? What can man offer to society, what can he expect from it? What follows earthly life? . . . What does the Church think of man? What recommendations seem needful for the upbuilding of contemporary society? What is the ultimate significance of human activity throughout the world?[33]

These questions are typical of the "anthropological turn" which was taken by official Catholicism at the Council. To ask "What is man?" is, at least implicitly and among other things, to ask "What is reason?" *Gaudium et Spes* and the subsequent official documents all proceed with their analysis of social moral questions and human rights with an awareness that their "reasonings" are under the influence of limits and perspectives established socially, technologically and methodologically.

The clearest evidence for this shift from the confident evaluation of the power of reason in the neo-scholastic period to the more tentative understanding of its scope in the more recent documents is the treatment of the relation of Christianity and culture in *Gaudium et Spes*. Like Vatican I, Vatican II refused to absorb all human achievement into a theological or religious empire. Not all questions can be answered by theology. But Vatican II made a significant variation in this consistent theme in Roman Catholic theology when it couched its argument in terms of a "proper autonomy" for culture rather than the relative autonomy of reason. In the following passage the attempt to maintain the basic theological point of view of the neo-scholastic approach while shifting to a cultural perspective is evident:

> This sacred Synod, therefore, recalling the teaching of the First Vatican Council, declares that there are "two orders of knowledge" which are distinct, namely, faith and reason. It declares that the Church does not indeed forbid that "when the human arts and sciences are practiced they use their own principles and their proper method, each in its own domain." Hence, "acknowledging this just liberty," this sacred Synod affirms the legitimate autonomy of human culture and especially the sciences.[34]

The shift here is not merely terminological. It involves a reconception of the intellectual method by which official Catholicism intends to go about addressing basic questions of the moral life. The shift can be clarified by comparing the previously cited notion of reason set forth in *Rerum Novarum* with that of culture found in *Gaudium et Spes*. *Rerum Novarum:*

> [M] an, fathoming *by his faculty of reason* matters without

> number, linking the future with the present, and being master of his own acts, guides his ways under the eternal law and the power of God, whose providence governs all things. Wherefore, it is in his power to exercise his choice not only as to matters that regard his present welfare, but also those which he deems may be for his advantage in time yet to come.[35]

Gaudium et Spes:

> The word *"culture" in its general sense* indicates all those factors by which man refines and unfolds his manifold spiritual and bodily qualities. It means his effort to bring the world itself under his control by his knowledge and his labor. It includes the fact that by improving customs and institutions he renders social life more human both within the family and in the civic community. Finally it is a feature of culture that throughout the course of time man expresses, communicates, and conserves in his works great spiritual experiences and desires, so that these may be of advantage to the progress of many, even of the whole human family.
>
> Hence it follows that human culture necessarily has a historical and social aspect and that the word "culture" often takes on a sociological and ethnological sense. It is in this sense that we speak of a plurality of cultures.[36]

In the neo-scholastic documents it is "reason" which gives persons the power to make history, to understand their social relationships, to be self-determining and to be obedient to God's law without loss of personhood and freedom. In *Gaudium et Spes* these functions are attributed to culture. The significant difference between these two formulations is twofold. First, culture is a possession of social groups in history, where reason is viewed as an individual characteristic of the person which can reach timeless truths. Second, *Gaudium et Spes* explicitly recognizes the existence of a plurality of cultures whereas the neo-scholastic documents speak in terms of a single reason possessed by all.

It is the recognition of the pluralism of human self-understandings, a pluralism due to the exigencies of social, technological and methodological diversification, that has stimulated the strong new emphasis on the importance of theological and religious belief in the Conciliar and post-Conciliar ethic. Affirming that culture is a pluralistic reality implies that it is no longer possible to speak of simple *agreement* or *disagreement* between the many dimensions of human self-understanding and religious faith. The various perspectives on human existence provided by diverse elements in culture are partial and their interrelations with each other are oblique and at times incommensurable. To speak of a harmonization between faith and reason as if reason were a unified reality would thus oversimplify what is in fact a very complex relationship.

The Council has recognized that the role played by religious belief in the formation of a moral framework is different from that played by social analyses, political theories and philosophies. These enter into the formulation of a theory of human rights, for example, in a way determined by their own methods and substantive limits. In Vatican II and subsequent documents the harmony between the religious and non-religious dimensions of the theory of rights is not a harmony of substantive conclusions but rather of methodological complementarity.

How this complementarity is conceived can be seen from noting the claims which are made for the role of religion in social existence by the documents. In the Declaration on the Relationship of the Church to Non-Christian Religions *(Nostra Aetate)* the Council set forth a notion of the role played by religion in human self-understanding. The questions to which religions respond are ultimate questions of meaning.

> Men look to the various religions for answers to those profound mysteries of the human condition which, today even as in olden times, deeply stir the human heart: What is a man? What is the meaning and purpose of our life? What is goodness and what is sin? What gives rise to our sorrows and to what intent? Where lies the path to true happiness? What is the truth about death, judgment and retribution beyond the grave? What, finally, is that ultimate and unutterable mystery which engulfs our being, and whence we take our rise, and whither our journey leads us?[37]

These ultimate questions are of a different nature than those which are approached through the methods of social science and even philosophy. They are questions which seek answers about the relationship between human existence and what lies simultaneously at its center and beyond its limits. They cannot be answered by forms of human thought which focus their attention *solely* on the diverse structures and fragmentary interpretations of human life alone. Even atheistic beliefs are the result of a grappling with questions of this all-encompassing sort and thus of a scrutiny of what might be beyond the limits of the knowledge attainable by specialized forms of non-religious thought.[38]

These ultimate beliefs about the world and the place of human persons in it are linked with the patterns of moral life in the great historical religions. Both implicitly and explicitly, these ultimate beliefs shape the limits and the directions of behavior for their adherents. In the words of the Council: "Religions to be found everywhere strive variously to answer the restless searchings of the human heart by proposing 'ways' which consist of teachings, rules of life, and sacred ceremonies."[39] These "ways" of living, though not exclusively limited to the moral life of persons in society, clearly include the moral life. Through doctrines, the example and teaching of Jesus Christ, and the life it shares in the Church, Christianity fits this description of a religion. Through these it offers both a vision of the ultimate meaning and goal of human existence and a "way" toward the realization of this meaning and the attainment of this goal.

This contribution of Christian faith to the moral life derives chiefly from the vision of the place of the human person in the world which Christianity provides. The treatment of the dignity of the human person in *Gaudium et Spes* is squarely theological. Persons are images of God. They attain freedom and liberation through the redemptive activity of God. All material reality, including the human body, is a creature of God and thus to be valued as essentially good. The fulfillment of the human quest for wisdom comes from the gift of the Holy Spirit. God is present in the heart and conscience of the person, a fact which gives the person an incalculable worth. Persons are destined to everlasting life with God beyond death. The shared life of persons in society is a reflection of the Trinitarian union of persons in the Godhead. God calls persons together to form a "people" and thus the fulfillment of their being is in love and communion with one another. Human activity, labor and industry are an image and participation in the creative activity of God. The tendency to deify human activity and to stake all hope on human progress can be overcome only by receiving all goods as gifts coming from the hand of God.[40]

These religious and theological dimensions of human existence in history are all appealed to in the development of the neo-scholastic ethic of the earlier documents, as we have seen above. The uniqueness of the Conciliar treatment lies in the fact that their role as interpretative keys for the understanding of the demands of human dignity in the face of cultural, social and intellectual pluralism has become both fully explicit and methodologically central. *Gaudium et Spes* states its radically theological approach to the dignity of the person in these words:

> The truth is that only in the mystery of the incarnate Word does the mystery of man take on light. For Adam, the first man, was a figure of Him who was to come, namely Christ the Lord. Christ, the final Adam, by the revelation of the mystery of the Father and His love, fully reveals man to man himself and makes his supreme calling clear. . . . Pressing upon the Christian, to be sure, are the need and the duty to battle against evil through manifold tribulations and even to suffer death. But, linked with the paschal mystery and patterned on the dying Christ, he will hasten forward to resurrection in the strength which comes from hope.
>
> All this holds good not only for Christians, but for all men of good will in whose hearts grace works in an unseen way. For, since Christ died for all men, and since the ultimate vocation of man is in fact one and divine, we ought to believe that the Holy Spirit in a manner known only to God offers to every man the possibility of being associated with this paschal mystery.[41]

In this passage the major theological development of the Council which has direct ethical implications is set forth. The Christian faith provides a vision of the person which forms the foundation of the moral life. All the Christian doctrines and symbols contribute to the formation of this vision, which is unified and focused in the person and work of Jesus Christ. The nature, dignity and destiny of all human persons are a participation in and image of the nature, dignity and destiny of Jesus Christ. The "way" of the Christian life is the way followed by Christ: love for his fellow humans, even to the point of suffering and death. It is this "way"—the way of the paschal mystery from life through death to resurrection—which leads to the attainment of that destiny which is made possible in Christ. The ethic which derives from this theological vision is thus at once theologically Christological, ontologically universal and epistemologically both distinctive and open to insight from all human sources, both those explicitly Christian and those not.[42]

The concrete implications of this way of linking the central theological foundations of Christian faith with the structures of human existence and dignity have become evident in the practical documents issued since the Council. These documents recognize the differentiation and pluralism of the present cultural situation. They then appeal to the theological doctrines and religious symbols of Christianity to help clarify the basic demands of human dignity. *Populorum Progressio* states that its conclusions are derived from the method set forth by the Council:

> Since the Church is situated in the midst of men, she therefore "has the duty of studying the signs of the times and of interpreting them in light of the Gospel." Consequently since the nobler aspirations of the Church are joined with those of men and she is afflicted with great sorrow because their hopes frequently turn out to be in vain, she therefore desires to assist their greatest fulfillment and for this reason offers to them what she alone possesses, that is a view of man and of human affairs in their totality.[43]

This claim to a total view of human affairs is not a claim to knowledge of all that there is to be known about social, economic, political and scientific matters. It is rather a claim that from the Gospel and the doctrines of the Christian faith, Christians possess the key by which the "signs of the times" can be properly interpreted. This totality is thus methodological, not substantive. Arrival at substantive conclusions depends on the full employment of the scientific and cultural resources which are available at any period in history. These resources are then to be organized, criticized and transformed in a dialectical way by the believer relying on the insights gained from the Christian faith. *Octogesima Adveniens* describes this interpretative process this way:

> The Church, in fact, travels forward with humanity and shares its lot in the setting of history. At the same time that she announces to men the Good News of salvation in Christ, she clarifies their activity in the light of the Gospel and in this way helps them to correspond to God's plan of love and to realize the fullness of their aspirations.[44]

The Synod document, *Justice in the World,* contains what is perhaps the most explicit enunciation of the method of work:

> The uncertainty of history and the painful convergences in the ascending path of the human community direct us to sacred history. There God has revealed Himself to us, and made known to us, as it is brought progressively to realization, His plan of liberation and salvation which is once and for all fulfilled in the Paschal Mystery of Christ. Action on behalf of justice and participation in the transformation of the world fully appear to us as a constitutive dimension of the preaching of the Gospel, or, in other words, of the Church's mission for the redemption of the human race and its liberation from every oppressive structure.[45]

The method here is clear. Christian faith helps clarify the historical demands of human dignity. At the same time, the moral task of humankind is entirely human. Discovery of its demands must rely fully on all available human resources. Thus Christian faith and human culture are both "constitutive dimensions" of this human task.

It is this methodology which forms the links between the neo-scholastic and post-Conciliar periods of the official tradition. In both phases theological understandings of the person establish the foundational norm of human dignity and specify its general content. Also, in both phases, philosophical and social scientific knowledge is used to spell out more specifically the demands of this human dignity in the concrete historical moment. The difference between the two periods stems from the recognition of pluralism in the cultural and intellectual situation of modern society which emerged at the Council.

Such de facto acceptance of the reality of pluralism has made it impossible for the Roman Catholic tradition to maintain its claim to a privileged insight into the meaning and demands of human dignity without making the ultimate sources of this insight more explicit than they were in the neo-scholastic period. In a society which was culturally suffused with Christian belief such explicitness was unnecessary. There is a paradoxical quality to this development. The ontological claim made by the Conciliar and post-Conciliar documents has been strengthened. An ontological relation to God and Jesus Christ is taken to be the foundation of the dignity of all persons, whether Christian or not. The more recent documents are much less ready to appeal to a distinction between a natural dignity of the person known from reason and a supernatural elevation of the person through grace known from revelation. In linking theology and anthropology through Christology, the recent documents make a distinctively Christian claim about the ontological constitution of all persons and about all dimensions of human existence, both religious and secular.

However, the epistemological claims made by the tradition have been in a sense more cautious and nuanced since the Council. It has been recognized that Catholicism cannot presume to have ready answers to all concrete questions of social morality or solutions which will be immediately evident to all reasonable people. Appeal to Christian doctrines and symbols to clarify and interpret concrete social questions means that official Catholicism has recognized that it is proceeding on the basis of a non-universal form of moral reasoning. The result of this recognition is that the ontological universalism present in the tradition must be accompanied by a kind of epistemological humility.

The rights of *all* human persons are the concern of Christians because they are rooted in universal human dignity. The human rights of all persons are a special concern of *Christians* precisely because of their ontological foundation in the reality of Jesus Christ. Thus official Catholicism, both in theory and in recent practice, has allied itself with growing attempts in secular society to specify and defend human rights. At the same time it has been more explicit in its appeal to theological warrants for its activity in the human rights sphere. In the words of the Council, "By virtue of the gospel committed to her, the Church proclaims the rights of man. She acknowledges and greatly esteems the dynamic movements of today by which these rights are everywhere fostered."[46] At the same time the concrete rights of persons are specified only with the assistance of the often fragmentary but nonetheless indispensable help of philosophical and social scientific reflection.

A New Approach to Pluralism and Conflict

We can conclude that it would be appropriate to characterize the approach of the most recent phase of the Catholic rights tradition as a *dialogically universalist ethic* rather than a natural law ethic. We might also call it an ethic of *pluralistic theological realism*. It is dialogic and pluralistic in its reliance on both the plural methods of the various human sciences and on the religious beliefs and doctrines of Christianity. It is theological in its ontological roots. And it is realistic and universalist in its epistemological claims to be seeking knowledge of the really existing structure of the dignity of every person and the ethical demands of this dignity.

The changed theological perspectives of the Conciliar and post-Conciliar periods have important ethical consequences, which are only gradually becoming apparent. Our analysis shows that the most recent documents grant a central though not exclusive position to Christian faith in the development of a Christian social ethic and understanding of human rights. The religious symbols and theological doctrines of Christianity establish the direction in which Christians should look in the attempt to develop both a theory of human rights and strategic set of priorities for their implementation. It is not presumed that such a theory and strategy are attainable by appeal to philosophical, empirical or social reason alone. The social and ideological pluralism of contemporary culture reveals that the circle of reason concerning human rights does not quite close. The interrelationship and interdependence of persons in society, therefore, cannot be accounted for fully by a theory of rights which is simultaneously fully universal and fully secular. This acknowledgment has opened the way for ecumenical rapprochement with Protestant churches in the effort to secure the dignity and rights of all.[47]

It is this acknowledgment which has brought the Christian norm of love to the forefront in the most recent phase of the Catholic rights tradition. All the doctrines and symbols of the Christian faith—creation of all persons by the one God, the universal graciousness of God toward all, the redemption of all by Christ, and the call of all persons to share in the mystery of Christ's death and resurrection—all these are the foundation of a conception of mutual love and human solidarity that is richer than any philosophical or empirical discussion of the mutual obligations of human beings toward each other, whether liberal or Marxist. It is deeper precisely because it is based on a claim about the ultimate meaning of human community. This religious perspective is leading the Catholic rights theory to an intensified emphasis on human solidarity as the precondition for any adequate theory of human rights. It is moving social rights to the center of recent Catholic discussions of human rights. Those rights which guarantee access of all to participation in the political, economic and cultural life of society have a priority in the most recent phase to the Catholic tradition. Similarly, the doctrines and symbols of the Christian faith lead to a notion of community which especially emphasizes care for the weak and the needy. When the claims of diverse groups in society conflict, the tradition increasingly grants priority to the needs of the weak over the desires and unimpeded liberty of the powerful. Christian faith and love, therefore, continually challenge, transform, heal and perfect the understanding of human rights which the tradition brings to the current debate. In so doing Christian faith does not dissolve conflict by appealing to a nonexistent harmony. Rather, it brings about new understandings of the way different human rights are to be prioritized when they make competing claims.

The appeal to religious beliefs in no way undercuts the importance of philosophical, empirical and social reason in the theory of rights and more general social ethic. The post-Conciliar discussions have not abandoned the use of philosophical reason so much admired in *Pacem in Terris* by philosophers such as Cranston. These discussions do imply, however, that it is not possible to formulate a single secular theory of rights and social justice which fully grasps the ultimate significance and concrete dimensions of human dignity in a definitive way. Thus the developments we have detected in the recent Catholic discussions point toward an increasing acceptance of the inevitability of conflict on the philosophical and ideological levels as well as on the level of politics and social life. The Conciliar and post-Conciliar official documents have become much more disposed to view the human rights theory as in need of continual reformulation and development on the basis of knowledge provided by the human sciences. This is especially true of strategies for the promotion of human rights which by their nature are socially conditioned and rooted in an analysis of social conflict. Through the use of social-scientific and philosophical reason, however, the Catholic tradition continues to address all persons of good will. The development of the theory of human rights and of strategies for their implementation depends on dialogue in the midst of these conflicts.

In the chapters which follow we will turn to a more detailed analysis of how Christian faith and love might become a source for the renewal of the Roman Catholic approach to human rights. The shifts in theological perspective which occurred at the Council have important consequences for the tradition's understanding of the place of conflict in society and for the appropriate strategic response to this conflict. The explicitation of these consequences will aid in the continuing renewal of the Catholic rights theory.

NOTES

1. See, for example, *RN,* no. 40, *DIM,* no. 6, *GS,* no. 12.

2. *PT,* no. 3.

3. *PT,* no. 9.

4. *GS,* no. 12.

5. Maurice Cranston, "Pope John XXIII on Peace and the Rights of Man," p. 380.

6. *PT,* no. 172.

7. Paul Tillich, untitled essay in Center for the Study of Democratic Institutions, *Pacem in Terris: Papers on Peace,* no. 4, "To Live as Men: The Anatomy of Peace," p. 18. The same theme can be found in several more recent Protestant discussions of human rights. See, for example, David Jenkins, "Theological Inquiry Concerning Human Rights: Some Questions, Hypotheses and Theses," *Ecumenical Review* XXVII (1975), pp. 101-102; Allen O. Miller, ed., *A Christian Declaration on Human Rights,* (Grand Rapids, MI: Eerdmans, 1977 ch. 12, pp. 145-146.

8. Allen O. Miller, ed., *A Christian Declaration on Human Rights,* p. 144.

9 Strauss, *Natural Rights and History* (Chicago: University of Chicago Press, 1953), p. 164.

10. Frederick A. Olafson, "Two Views of Pluralism: Liberal and Catholic," *Yale Review* 51 (1962), p. 531.

11. Jürgen Moltmann, "A Christian Declaration on Human Rights," in Allen O. Miller, ed., *A Christian Declaration on Human Rights,* p. 130. For similar recent efforts to ground human rights theologically see Heinz-Eduard Tödt, "Theological Reflections on the Foundations of Human Rights," *Lutheran World* 1/1977, pp. 45–58, and the study document entitled "Theological Aspects of Human Rights," prepared by the Theological Studies Department of the Federation of Protestant Churches in the German Democratic Republic, *WCC Exchange,* no. 6 (December, 1977).

12. See, for example, *RN,* nos. 19-23; *Lib,* no. 13; *AP,* no. 29, *Diut,* no. 11; *ID,* nos. 3-5; *DIM,* nos. 29 and 41; *QA,* nos. 42-43; *DR,* nos. 14, 27 and 29; Pius XII, Pentecost Address, 1941, in Yzermans, I, pp. 28-33, Christmas Address 1942, in Yzermans, II, pp. 59-63, Address of Dec. 6, 1953, in Yzermans, I, pp. 270-71.

13. See *DIM,* no. 97 *QA,* no. 11; *DR,* no. 25, *CCC,* no. 30; Pius XII, Pentecost Address, 1941, in Yzermans, I, p. 28, Address of March 23, 1952, in Yzermans, I, p. 198.

14. *AP,* no. 8.

15. *AP,* no. 9. See *Lib,* no. 27. For an excellent analysis of this line of reasoning in Leo XIII see James Collins, "Leo XIII and the Philosophical Approach to Modernity," in Edward T. Gargan, ed., *Leo XIII and*

the Modern World (New York: Sheed and Ward, 1961), pp. 179-209.

16. In a recent essay James M. Gustafson has argued that "In Western religions, their documents, their histories and the experience of their communities, religion and morality are joined together, intertwined, commingled, indeed in some instances even unified. Further, because of this comingling and unification, the concept of morality itself evades the precise definition and usage that philosophers often seek." "Religion and Morality from the Perspective of Theology," Gene Outka and John P. Reeder. *Religion and Morality* (Garden City, N.Y.: Doubleday, 1973), pp. 125-154. Gustafson argues that in Judaism and Christianity the attributes and qualities of God include notions which are properly moral. In the analysis which is given here I am indebted to Gustafson for my basic approach. It should become clear in what follows that such a linkage between religion and morality is present in the neo-scholastic documents of official Roman Catholic ethics. The supposition that this is not the case is one of the oversimplifications which has resulted from seeing only the discontinuities produced in the tradition at Vatican II.

17. *UA,* no. 28.

18. *RN,* nos. 23-24.

19. *IP,* nos. 14 and 19: *UA,* nos. 28-31.

20. See, e.g., *RN,* no. 16; *Inscrut,* nos. 5 and 6; *Diut,* no. 3; *CCC,* no. 28; *MBS,* no. 34; *DR,* no. 27; Pius XII, Christmas Address 1942, in Yzermans, II, p. 52; Address of Feb. 20, 1946, in Yzermans, I, p. 79; Christmas Address 1952, in Yzermans, II, p. 202.

21. See, e.g., *QA,* no. 9; Pius XII, Pentecost Address 1941, in Yzermans, I, p. 28.

22. The relation between beliefs and moral claims is not, however, illogical. The logic involved is more akin to that which finds its primary exemplification in the rational processes employed in legal and rhetorical argument than that found in mathematics or, perhaps, the physical sciences. For two very helpful treatments of this diversity of the types of rational arguments see Stephen Toulmin, "The Layout of Arguments" in his *The Uses of Argument* (Cambridge: Cambridge University Press, 1969), pp. 127-45, and Chaim Perelman, *Justice* (New York: Random House, 1967), esp. pp. 58-70 and 91-110. These analyses show that a logical or rational relation between religion and morality can exist without this relation being subject to the criteria of strict entailment. We are arguing here that such a less narrowly defined notion of the logical relation between religion and morality is at the heart of the neo-scholastic method.

23. The power of symbols to uncover the ontological structure of the real has been treated with great insight by Iris Murdoch in her article, "Vision and Choice in Morality," contained in the collection edited by Ian T. Ramsey, *Christian Ethics and Contemporary Philosophy* (London: SCM, 1966), pp. 195-218 and in her more recent book *The Sovereignty of Good* (New York: Schocken, 1971). Also, an extremely

interesting treatment of the same question by a theologian is Langdon Gilkey's "Symbols, Meaning and the Divine Presence," *Theological Studies* 35 (June 1974), pp. 259–267.

24. *DR*, no. 19.

25. This understanding of the love/justice relationship in neo-scholastic social thought is discussed in more detail in Chapter Four.

26. *GS*, no. 4. See *GS*, no. 54.

27. *GS*, no. 4. See *MM*, no. 206.

28. *GS*, no. 63.

29. *PP*, nos. 8 and 9.

30. *JW*, no. 9.

31. *GS*, nos. 5, 36 and 54; *OA*, no. 40.

32. *OA*, nos. 38-39.

33. *GS*, nos. 10 and 11.

34. *GS*, no. 59. The citations are from Vatican I, *Constitution on the Catholic Faith*, DS 3015, 3019, with a reference to *QA*.

35. *RN*, no. 7. Emphasis added.

36. *GS*, no. 53. Emphasis added.

37. *Nostra Aetate*, no. 1.

38. See *GS*, no. 21 and Paul VI's *Ecclesiam Suam*, nos. 103 and 108. A similar interpretation of religious language as limit language can be found in David Tracy, *Blessed Rage for Order: The New Pluralism in Theology* (New York: Seabury 1975). In Tracy's words, religious language "can be analyzed as both expressive of certain 'limits-to' our ordinary experience (e.g., finitude, contingency, or radical transience) and disclosure of certain fundamental structures of our existence beyond (or alternatively, grounding to) that ordinary experience" (p. 93).

39. *Nostra Aetate*, no. 2. The Council's understanding of religion is remarkably similar to that proposed by Clifford Geertz. Geertz has influenced my interpretation of the relation between religion and culture and thus my reading of the developing Catholic tradition. See his well known essay, "Religion as a Cultural System," in Donald R. Cutler, ed., *The Religious Situation: 1968* (Boston: Beacon Press 1968), pp. 639–688).

40. *GS*, nos. 12-18, 24, 32, 34 and 37.

41. *GS*, no. 22. See *GS*, nos. 10, 38 and 45.

42. Josef Ratzinger sees the passage of *Gaudium et Spes* quoted immediately above as the highpoint of the document. "The attempt to pursue discussion with non-believers on the basis of 'humanitas' here culminates in the endeavor to interpret being human Christologically and so attain the 'resolutio in theologiam' which, it is true, also means 'resolutio in hominem' (provided the sense of 'homo' is understood deeply enough). We are probably justified in saying that here for the first time in an official document of the magisterium a new type of completely Christocentric theology appears. On the basis of Christ this dares to present theology as anthropology and only becomes radically theological by including man in discourse about God by way of Christ, thus manifesting

the deepest unity of theology." "The Dignity of the Human Person," in Vorgrimler, ed., *Commentary,* vol. V p. 159. For a concise statement of Karl Rahner's understanding of the relationship between anthropology, theology and Christology, see his "Christian Humanism," in *Theological Investigations,* vol. IX, pp. 187-204.

43. *PP,* no. 13. The citation is from *GS,* no. 4.

44. *OA,* no. 1.

45. *JW,* no. 6.

46. *GS,* no. 41. See *GS,* no. 26; *DH,* no. 12; *PP,* no. 32; *JW,* no. 39.

47. The interpretations of these developments in Catholic rights theory are markedly parallel to conclusions reached in a study of Protestant efforts to "decode" human rights language theologically. See "Theological Aspects of Human Rights," *WCC Exchange,* no. 6 (December 1977).

Part Three
Renewal

Chapter Four
Claims in Conflict

As we have seen in three previous chapters, the Roman Catholic theory of rights has incorporated the rights stressed by both the liberal democratic and the socialist traditions. Because its distinctive approach to the foundation of human rights stresses both the dignity of the human person and the essentially social nature of that dignity, the Catholic rights theory has refused to give exclusive emphasis to either civil and political liberties or to social and economic needs. Especially since Pope John and Vatican II, the tradition has emphasized the integral relatedness and interconnection of all basic human rights. This interrelation of rights was made most explicit in the 1971 Synod's stress on the right to development, which it defined as "the dynamic interpenetration of all those fundamental human rights upon which the aspirations of individuals and nations are based."[1] The concern which these emphases represent is a concern to avoid all premature closure of the sphere of rights.

In the world of action and policy-making, however, such inclusiveness raises several important questions. Has the theoretical inclusiveness of this approach to rights been bought at the cost of abstract generality? Has the emphasis on the interconnection between all human rights made it impossible to establish priorities in a world where not all desirable goods are immediately and simultaneously realizable? Does the desire to reconcile and harmonize all the various human rights really betray an inability to admit the reality of social conflict and the need for making hard choices?[2]

Though the foundation of the Catholic understanding of rights has emerged clearly from our examination of the tradition, the concrete interrelations between rights need fuller exploration. The same is true of the practical means which the theory proposes as means for the implementation of rights. The reality of social conflict is central to both of these issues.

This chapter will explore what resources the Catholic social tradition contains that can provide practical guidance in dealing with conflicts between rights claims. An examination of the tradition from this point of view reveals that Catholic teaching has tended to minimize the presence of conflict between competing rights. This has been so because of a desire to keep all dimensions of human dignity—both political and civil liberties and social and economic needs—within the domain of human rights. Also, until quite recently the tradition has relied on a model of social interaction which highlights the structural harmonies and organic unities of social life while minimizing institutional strains and social conflict. Finally, it has been the result of a Christian conviction that love can be a source of reconciliation and conflict resolution.

For these reasons, a simple retrieval of the tradition's approach to the interrelation and institutionalization of rights will not be sufficient for our purposes. If the Catholic tradition is to make a vigorous contribution to the contemporary debate on these two points it will have to be the contribution of a renewed tradition. An important renewal of the theological foundations of the Catholic rights theory was stimulated by the recognition of the reality of social and ideological pluralism. A similar renewal in the practical implementation of human rights will depend on overcoming the tradition's propensity for minimizing the conflicts which exist between diverse rights claims.

Despite this propensity, however, the tradition does contain several very important resources which have been used in addressing problems of rights conflict. Foremost among these resources is the tradition's understanding of the principles of justice. The documents repeatedly appeal to the notion of justice to specify how the exercise of rights by some persons is limited by the rights of others. Justice is the moral norm governing "the claims and counter-claims of historical existence." [3] The first part of this chapter will explore ways in which the tradition's understanding of the principles of justice can contribute to an adequate approach to the problem of rights conflict.

Future development of the tradition will depend on a revision of the models of society which shape the tradition's interpretation of how persons and groups actually interact. The second section of the chapter will suggest that Catholic thinking on the institutional implications of justice needs to be revised. The proposal involves a shift in the way social and political institutions—and therefore instrumental rights—are conceived. It calls for a shift from a paradigm which emphasizes their role as instruments of the organic harmony of social life to one which highlights their function as instruments of greater equality in situations characterized by inequalities of material well-being, freedom and power.

Finally, the notion of Christian love has been closely connected with the principles of justice throughout the tradition. At times the appeal to love has masked the reality of genuine conflict. In the recent documents, however, reliance on love as a norm of social morality has been both greater and different in kind from that characteristic of the pre-Conciliar period. This new stress on the centrality of love is an important result of the shift in the tradition's understanding of the relation between the theological, philosophical and social scientific throught which was analyzed in the previous chapter. Since Vatican II, the ideological potential of both philosophical theories of justice and scientific models of social interaction has been recognized in a new way. In this situation the tradition has increasingly appealed to Christian love to direct attention to the actual needs of persons in society and to the ways in which they are being excluded from communal participation. This development has meant renewed insistance that the scale of justice must not be constructed in a way which enables it to be used as a defense of privileged social position or of an unequal distribution of personal or group power. Neither can it be used as a defense of private advantage in the face of public need. In other words, the increasing reliance on the norm of love has led to a much more egalitarian approach to the problem of rights conflict. The third section of this chapter will analyze this development and suggest how it might be carried further.

RIGHTS AND JUSTICE

The opening paragraphs of Leo XIII's *Rerum Novarum* reveal the central role played by the principles of justice in the

Catholic tradition's approach to the problem of conflicting rights claims. This encyclical began with a description of the conflicts caused by the process of industrialization and modernization—conflicts between workers and capitalists, rich and poor, conflicts between ideologies, social theories and moral visions. The encyclical's goal was to address these conflicts by clarifying both the demands of justice and the interrelationship between the rights of the conflicting groups. In the encyclical's words:

> The elements of the conflict now raging are unmistakable. . . . So have we thought it expedient now to speak on the conditions of the working classes . . . in order that no misapprehension may exist as to the principles which truth and justice dictate for its settlement. The discussion is not easy, nor is it void of danger. It is no easy matter to define the relative rights and mutual duties of the rich and of the poor, of capital and labor.[4]

These words show how the notion of rights and the principles of justice are correlative in the tradition's approach to social conflict. In order to specify what rights in fact exist, it is necessary to engage in some form of comparison and weighing of the competing claims of the individuals and groups which compose society. This comparison must be based on the genuine dignity and true needs of those involved ("truth") and on the relative weight of the claims emerging from this dignity and need in relation to the weight of the competing claims of others ("justice"). The entire theory of rights is developed within the framework of a complementary theory of justice. Rights represent claims to those things which are due individuals. The notion of justice is an indispensable means in the process of judging which of these claims takes priority over others in situations of conflict. The language of rights, therefore, focuses on the dignity, liberty and needs of all persons in society regarded disjunctively or one at a time. The language of justice, on the other hand, focuses on the dignity, liberty and needs of all persons regarded conjunctively or as bound by obligations and duties to one another.[5]

The principles of justice are not appealed to by the tradition to resolve conflicts of rights according to an extrinsic standard. Rather, the intrinsic correlation of rights and justice reflects the fact that all genuine rights exist in an ordered relationship with each other.[6] It is the task of the principles of justice to make this order explicit.

Over the past hundred years, Catholicism has gradually developed a complex theory of justice to handle this problem of ordering and interrelating rights. The theory understands justice as the rendering to all persons what is due them. The most general content of the notion of justice is stated in the ancient principle of *suum cuique*—to each his own.[7] This principle is exceedingly general, however. The concrete determination of just what is due and to whom it is due demands that the concept of justice be given greater specific content. To this end, three modalities or types of justice are employed throughout the documents: commutative, distributive and social justice.[8]

The division of these types of justice is made on the basis of the kinds of social interaction which they govern. Commutative justice is concerned with the relationships which bind individual to individual in the sphere of private transactions. Distributive and social justice, on the other hand, are concerned with public or political life, that is with the relationships which exist between society as a whole and its individual members or sub-groups. Distributive justice determines how public social goods are to be allocated to individuals or groups. Conversely, social justice specifies how the activities of individuals and groups are to be aggregated so that they converge to create the social good.[9]

It is precisely in these different spheres of interaction between persons that conflicting rights claims arise. Conflicts within each sphere are addressed by the type of justice which governs that sphere. For example, conflicts regarding rights to remuneration for work or rights arising from contracts or promises are conflicts in the sphere of private interaction. Commutative justice is the standard employed by the tradition to adjudicate these conflicts. The core of the concept of commutative justice to which the tradition appeals in addressing such conflicts are the equal dignity and freedom of the persons involved. Leo XIII affirmed that a worker has a just claim to a wage equal in value to his labor.

This is so because both employer and worker are equal in dignity. This personal equality implies that when persons enter freely into an agreement to exchange work for wages, the agreement is equally binding on both parties. Commutative justice thus governs wage agreements by a standard of *strict equality*. Neither worker nor employer possesses a status which would justify any sort of privileged claim in the wage-for-work transaction. It is in this sense that one should interpret Pius XI's statement that the "mutual relations between capital and labor must be determined according to the laws of strictest justice, called commutative justice."[10] In this context, "strict" refers to what Aristotle would call an "arithmetical" proportion: the wage/labor exchange creates an obligation which is equally binding on worker and employer and the exchange itself must be one of strict equality.[11] The same standard of strict equality is normative in other private interactions such as promises, contracts and property transactions. Conflicting claims are to be adjudicated according to the standard of arithmetic equality.

The notion of commutative justice, then, is based on the transcendental equality of all human persons in their direct and unmediated relations with other persons. As a pure "type" of justice it is not concerned with questions of social and political equality. As "man precedes the state" so the equality which is the standard of commutative justice precedes all differentiations between persons is based on their social or political positions. Nevertheless, though commutative justice is potentially a refuge for social reactionaries seeking to protect their self-interests by citing contracts or deeds to property, it need not have this effect. Indeed, Leo XIII and all of his successors have used the egalitarian core of the notion of commutative justice as a defense of the equal right of all persons to work. It has also been used to conclude that the payment of what are effectively slave wages is a fundamental denial of the rights of the worker, for the payment of such inadequate wages is a denial of the equal dignity of employer and employee. Strong appeals to commutative justice, therefore, can have progressive or reactionary effects depending on how one understands the structures of the larger society within which the appeals are made and how these structures influence and shape human relations in the private sphere. If one should conclude that a society is so organized as to make quality in contracts impossible, as Leo XIII and Pius XI did, then the egalitarian core of commutative justice will become a demand for social change.

It is clear, therefore, that the concern with equality in private transactions can generate only a partial account of the order of rights which regulates human interrelationships in their richness and multiple dimensions. Taken alone, the standard of commutative justice gives only a partial response to the problem of conflicting claims. The uniqueness and dignity of human persons never exists in isolation from their relations with the larger community. The conjunction of persons in societies and communities is never simply an arithmetic sum. There are goods or values necessary for the realization of human dignity which transcend the sphere of private interaction and contract which is the concern of commutative justice. For example, such goods as political self-determination, participation in the economic productivity of an industrialized society, and enjoyment of one's cultural heritage can be obtained by an individual only through participation in the public life of society. No one creates a polity, an economy or a culture in private. Individuals come to share in these goods in a way that is mediated by political, economic and cultural structures.[12]

Such goods, in other words, are essentially public. Though they have moral significance only in relation to the dignity of individual persons, they are not created by any individual person acting alone or even through the activity of persons banding together through contract, consent or some other form of strictly autonomous choice. These goods are essentially relational. If they are to exist at all they must exist as shared. In Douglas Sturm's definition, the public good "is the good of the relationships through which the members of the community sustain one another, contribute to one another, and constitute a creative center for the ongoing life of the community." [13] Public goods, in other words, cannot be said properly to "belong" to any person as private property. They "belong" to individuals only because and to the extent that these individuals "belong" to society. Claims on these goods are claims to be permitted or enabled to participate in the life and activity of the communities which make their existence possible. These claims are the social rights schematized in Chapter Two: the rights to assembly, association, political participation, work, adequate health care, etc. They are called social rights because the goods to which they lay claim are conditions of public life in its various dimensions. The aggregate set of all such public goods, considered in their interrelatedness and mutual dependence, constitutes what the tradition calls the common good.

The norm of distributive justice is the standard used by the tradition to sort out the claims of individuals and groups to participation in and access to these public goods. A key text for understanding the conceptual framework within which the documents discuss questions of distribution appears in *Rerum Novarum:*

> As regards the State, the interests of all, whether high or low, are equal. The members of the working classes are citizens by nature and by the same right as the rich; they are real parts, living the life which makes up, through the family, the body of the commonwealth; and it need hardly be said that they are in every city very largely in the majority. It would be irrational to neglect one portion of the citizens and favor another, and therefore the public administration must duly and solicitously provide for the welfare and the comfort of the working classes; otherwise, that law of justice will be violated which ordains that each man shall have his due. To cite the words of St. Thomas Aquinas: "As the part and the whole are in a certain sense identical, so that which belongs to the whole in a sense belongs to the part." Among the many and grave duties of rulers who would do their best for the people, the first and chief is to act with strict justice—with that justice which is called distributive—toward each and every class alike.[14]

Several points should be noted about this passage. First, distributive justice is here referred to as *strict justice*. Pius XI's statement that commutative justice is strict justice, noted above, should not be read to imply that distributive justice is in some sense less binding than commutative justice. Both in Leo's discussions of distributive justice and in Pius XI's statement on commutative justice, "strictness" is directly linked to human equality. Here Leo affirms that all citizens have an equal claim to a share in public goods—"the interests of all, whether high or low, are equal."[15]

Second, the citation from St. Thomas makes it clear that distributive justice is not to be identified with what we might call "justice by division." The distribution envisioned here is not a dividing up of the public good into individual parcels which will then be dispersed to individuals one at a time. It is not an "arithmetic" standard. Public goods cannot be arithmetically divided, since they are essentially shared realities. For example, persons cannot share in the value of political self-determination except through active membership in the political community. Economic well-being depends not only on the arithmetic quantity of one's income but also on active engagement in the organized world of work and economic exchange. The claims or rights of individuals to share in public goods are realized by achieving access to and participation in social value, not by simply obtaining a "piece" of it. With regard to those goods which are essentially public, then, "the part and the whole are in a certain sense identical, so that which belongs to the whole in a sense belongs to the part."[16] The need for access to and participation in the public life of society, whether in the economic, political or cultural spheres, is a crucial factor in the tradition's approach to rights conflict.

More concretely, the notion of distributive justice has several components.[17] It involves the recognition of the right of all persons to have access to those public goods which are essential for the protection of their dignity in the actual conditions of social life. This means equality of opportunity for entry into the social, economic, cultural and political relationships which constitute the common good. Following Leo XIII, Pius XI argued in *Quadragesimo Anno* that the benefits of industrialization—values which are essentially public or social—should not be monopolized by a privileged class.[18] The argument here is based on the fact that the wealth produced by industrial progress is the product of both labor and capital. Moreover, the industrial system as a whole is sustained not merely by workers and capitalists, but by the entire community of persons who live under its influence. This implies that virtually all persons are at least indirect participants in the creation of industrial wealth.[19] Distributive justice, therefore, implies the right of all persons to share in all those goods which express, support and sustain the public life of society.

Consideration of human need is a second component in the determination of the demands of distributive justice. As Leo XIII argued with regard to both labor and property, there are forms of human interrelationship which are not only expressions of the collaborative exercise of personal freedom but which are also quite rigorously necessary for the preservation of human dignity.

> Man's labor necessarily bears two notes or characters. First of all, it is *personal,* inasmuch as the force which acts is bound up with the human personality and is the exclusive property of him who acts, and further, was given to him for his advantage. Secondly, man's labor is *necessary;* for without the result of labor a man cannot live, and self-preservation is a law of nature, which it is wrong to disobey. Now, were we to consider labor merely insofar as it is personal, doubtless it would be within the workman's right to accept any rate of wages whatsoever; for in the same way as he is free to work or not, so he is free to accept a small wage or even none at all. But our conclusion must be very different if, together with the personal element in a man's work, we consider the fact that work is also necessary for him to live: these two aspects of his work are separable in thought, but not in reality. . . . It necessarily follows that each one has a natural right to what is required in order to live.[20]

The principle of need is thus a necessary supplement to that of access and participation in determining the order of rights claims demanded by distributive justice. The fulfillment of human need is an essential aspect of the common good, for the resources of nature are given by God to the human race in common for the benefit of all its members. At the same time, since all social and economic structures are social products, they must be open to the participation of all persons.[21] Distributive justice will be realized when social patterns are so organized that they meet the minimum needs of all persons and permit all an equal opportunity to participate in the public activities which meet these needs. These claims take priority over claims arising from merit, private ownership, social status, or de facto political power.[22]

The principle of distributive justice *orders* fundamental human rights. In the economic sphere the rights of employers and owners are recognized and related to the rights of workers by commutative justice. However, distributive justice limits the rights of employers by the just claims of workers to minimum levels of wages and to participation in the economic life of society. The rights of the wealthy and of majorities in a society are similarly limited by the rights of the poor and of minorities to minimum economic levels and minimum levels of political self-determination. The function of distributive justice, therefore, is to insure that the rights of all are guaranteed in social, economic, political and cultural interaction. Distributive justice implies that it is not enough to guarantee core personal rights in private interactions in a merely formal way. The actual conditions of public life must also be taken into account in deciding how to adjudicate between competing claims. Distributive justice therefore demands that social rights be protected. It does this by granting priority to those rights which make claims to a share in public goods over claims which reinforce patterns that deny some persons all access to these goods. It also does so by limiting the exercise of the claims of those whose social power, wealth or status grant them privileged ability to make or implement claims. Distributive justice, in other words, sets limits to the validity of claims based on a simply formal notion of equality. The important result of this view is the conclusion that those claims which are recognized as valid by the norm of commutative justice such as freedom of contract and the right to private property may in fact be limited or restricted in scope by distributive justice. The exercise of personal rights by persons in privileged social positions may be limited in order to guarantee the social rights of those not so privileged. Commutative justice—the equality of rights in the private sphere—is not abolished by distributive justice but rather regulated by it in accordance with the structural realities of public life.[23]

In addition to the distribution of the public goods of a society to its individual members there is a complementary relation between person and society which is a concern of justice. This relation is discussed by the documents in their treatment of the third type of justice—social justice. Social justice is the measure which orders personal activities in a way which is suitable for the *production and protection* of the common good. It is an aggregative principle. In Pius XI's words, "It is of the very essence of social justice to demand from each individual all that is necessary for the common good." [24] In contrast with distributive considerations, the aggregative concerns which fall under social justice do not begin with the presupposition that public good already exists or will come to exist spontaneously. Social justice is a measure or ordering principle which seeks to bring into existence those social relationships which will guarantee the possibility of realizing the demands of distributive justice. This means that it calls for the creation of those social, economic and political conditions which are necessary to assure that the minimum human needs of all will be met and which will make possible social and political participation for all. In other words, social justice demands that the institutions of society be ordered in a way that makes it possible to protect the social and personal rights of all. The instrumental rights schematized in Chapter Two concretize and differentiate this demand.

As was pointed out in our review of the history of the tradition, the notion of social justice became prominent in the writings of Pius XI due to his increased appreciation of the importance of institutional or structural change in society. The distinctive characteristic of social justice is its concern with developing institutional organization. Together with its stress on the *creation* of public goods, this structural concern means that social justice is a standard which has its primary application in measuring the active ordering function of government. It seeks to create an order in which all persons realize those kinds of activity to which their human dignity makes rightful claim. In the words of *Quadragesimo Anno:*

> To that end all the institutions of public and social life must be imbued with the spirit of justice, and this justice must be truly operative. It must build up a juridical and social order able to pervade all economic activity.[25]

As a result, though social justice is concerned with ordering the activity of individuals and groups to produce the common good, its content is defined in terms of institutional structures, especially with deployment of institutional power in society. This content is specified and differentiated in terms of the instrumental rights to social security, juridical protection (due process and *habeas corpus*), freedom of information, etc. Because government is that power charged with the protection of rights and the guaranteeing of justice in society as a whole, the tradition appeals to social justice as the standard which orders conflicting rights through the use of juridical and political power.

Social justice, in other words, is not simply a theoretical moral standard. It is a practical guideline for the use of the instruments of power, especially governmental power. In commenting on the passage from Pius XI cited immediately above, Nell-Breuning has described this governmental or juridical concern of social justice:

> We see that the Pope attaches first importance to governmental and social institutions. . . . Social justice is a spiritual and intellectual guiding rule which does not act through itself, but assisted by a power. This power, according to Leo XIII and Pius XI, is the state. The right social and economic order is established by the supreme authority in society, which in turn is bound by the demands of social justice from which it draws all its legal authority to direct and regulate. In a properly regulated community, social justice finds its material realization in public institutions, and acts through public authorities or their representatives.
>
> The result of this social justice, always an efficient principle in public authority, shall, according to the Pope's statement, look first of all to social legislation: it shall bring about a legal social order that will result in the proper economic order . . . . In this sense social justice, as a spiritual

> and intellectual principle of the form of human society, becomes an institution in the constitution and laws of society.[26]

The institutionalization of justice takes place when both constitution and legislation place governmental power at the service of social rights and distributive justice. It takes place when a just order of rights is guaranteed instrumentally.

The norm of social justice thus makes claims on both individuals and governments. It demands that persons contribute to the creation of those institutions needed for the protection of the rights of all, and that these persons exercise their own rights within the limitations demanded by these institutional factors. It demands that governments guarantee the rights of citizens and, where necessary, limit the exercise of these rights in order that the dignity of all is protected.[27]

The personal and social rights of all persons provide the concrete criteria which guide the application of the standard of social justice. The minimum necessities of economic life determine a kind of base line which is continually referred to in discussion of social justice. The same is true of the rights which concern access to and participation in public goods. The procedures of government and the structures of social and economic life which are the concern of social justice are measured by these substantive claims of the dignity of the human person. Social justice is the norm of the procedural and structural order within which these claims exist.[28] It orders these claims by taking their institutional interrelationships into account.

Social justice, then, is a standard which seeks to guarantee human dignity by specifying forms of governmental intervention which are appropriate for the protection of minimum standards of well-being, access and participation for all individuals. These forms of intervention do not arise from some autonomous power of government over individual persons and their rights. Rather, the legitimacy of these interventions is the consequence of the fact that there is an institutional or political dimension to the dignity of all persons. The realization of social justice will occur when the institutional and juridical power of society is deployed in a way that meets minimum needs and guarantees political participation for all. The wealth and power of the privileged are limited by this more fundamental claim. Social justice, therefore, justifies governmental limitation of the accumulation of wealth or the exercise of political influence to the extent this is necessary for the institutionalization of basic economic and political rights for all.

In summary, there are three distinct but complementary notions of justice in the tradition—commutative, distributive and social. Commutative justice guarantees the equal dignity of persons in interpersonal or private transactions. In the concrete, however, commutative justice always exists within a social context, and the fulfillment of the particular rights claims of individuals is limited by the claims of all people to share in public goods to some minimum level. For example, the right to enter into contracts regarding wages is not a right of employers to pay a wage below the minimum necessary for the subsistence of the worker and his family. Similarly, rights to economic freedom or to the exercise of political influence are not unlimited claims. Distributive justice limits commutative justice and personal freedoms here. Distributive justice orders the exercise of competing rights claims in such a way that no one (or at least a minimum number of persons) is excluded from participation in those goods which are essentially social. Furthermore, the entire society is under obligation to create institutions which make the satisfaction of these demands of distributive justice possible. This demand is met through the society acting in a politically organized way—that is, through government. Social justice, therefore, is the ordering of rights through legislation and other forms of governmental activity. This governmental power to intervene and to coerce arises from the interdependent character of human existence and from the fact that some rights are claims on goods which are essentially public and which cannot be weighed out and distributed piecemeal. All three forms of justice taken together provide a general framework for adjudicating between competing rights claims and for assigning priorities for social and political action.

Social Models and Instrumental Rights

The principles of justice are important conceptual tools for addressing the problem of conflicting rights claims. They provide a language for discussing the interrelations between the personal, social and institutional aspects of human rights. They make it clear that the solution to the problem of rights conflict is not simply a matter of arranging the list of core personal rights (life, health, work, self-determination, etc.), as a hierarchy of values for sequential implementation. These norms of justice were developed by the tradition out of an awareness that the problem of rights conflict is simultaneously distributive and aggregative. It involves a complex interweaving of personal, social and institutional factors. For this reason all concrete solutions to the problem of rights conflict involve decisions about the proper form of interaction between these three spheres of action. In other words, the development of a full theory of the problem of rights conflict will depend on the use of a model of social organization. As John Rawls has put it, "Fully to understand a conception of justice we must make explicit the conception of social cooperation from which it derives." [29]

The problem of rights conflict, therefore, is a problem in social and political theory as well as a problem of normative ethics. In concrete action the balance between competing rights claims will be embodied in structured configurations of social and political power. The organizational means by which power is distributed and aggregated are highly significant in determining which claims will in fact be supported and which will not. There is a wide array of possible models of social interaction and power organization which might be employed in addressing the problem of rights conflict. The different models of social interaction adopted by pluralist democracy, state socialism, anarcho-syndicalism, corporatism and Fascism are at the root of their disagreements about the appropriate ways to institutionalize human rights. These disputes center on a debate about the proper place of the "megastructures" of power (the state, economic conglomerates, big labor and the growing professional bureaucracies) in relation to the roles of individuals and smaller groups.[30]

Fundamental to this debate is a disagreement about how different social agents can and should be interrelated. Efforts to defend human rights must necessarily assign relative weights to the activity and power of individual persons, to the action of the whole society organized by government, and to the action of intermediate groups such as families, local communities, labor unions, professional associations, etc. Disputes about conflicting rights claims are frequently rooted in disagreements about the relative social importance and capabilities of these diverse groups.[31]

In modern Catholic social thought this issue has been addressed by appealing to the "principle of subsidiarity." Some form of this principle can be found in nearly every major social document of the tradition since *Rerum Novarum*. It was given its classic formulation by Pius XI in *Quadragesimo Anno:*

> Just as it is wrong to take away from individuals what by their own ability and effort they can accomplish and commit it to the community, so it is an injury and at the same time both a serious evil and a perturbation of right order to assign to a larger and higher society what can be performed successfully by smaller and lower communities. This is a fixed and unchangeable principle most basic in social philosophy, immovable and unalterable. The reason is that all social activity, of its very power and nature, should supply help to the members of the social body, but may never destroy or absorb them.[32]

The principle states that government intervention is justified when it truly provides help *("subsidium")* to the persons and smaller communities which compose society. More importantly, however, the family, the neighborhood, the church, and both professional and labor groups all have a dynamic life of their own which must be respected by government. There are legitimate claims rooted in the dynamics and structure of these groups.

If a theory of rights does not take these claims into account it will, as Roberto Unger has put it, become "a language of rights as abstract opportunities to enjoy certain advantages rather than a language of the concrete and actual experience of social life." [33] The principle of subsidiarity is the Catholic tradition's shorthand expression for the importance of claims rising from the concrete experience of group life. It is an abbreviated way of stating the difference between society viewed as a heap or mass of individuals unrelated except through the state and society considered as a people who are related and active in many diverse kinds of associations. In the words of Pius XII:

> The state does not contain in itself and does not mechanically bring together in a given territory a shapeless mass of individuals. It is, and should in practice be, the organic and organizing unity of a real people. The people and a shapeless multitude (or, as it is called, "the masses") are two distinct concepts.[34]

Thus, according to the principle of subsidiarity, the power of government to intervene is real. It should be exercised to the extent necessary for the production of distributive and social justice. But it is a limited power. Both the scope and the limits of this intervention arise not only from the claims of individual persons but also from the need to insure that the multiple forms of human community are not obliterated by the power of the state.[35] *Rerum Novarum* stated the case both for intervention and for the limits of intervention with special reference to the family:

> We have said that the state must never absorb the individual or the family; both should be allowed free and untrammeled activity so far as it is consistent with the common good and the interests of others. . . . The limits of government intervention must be determined by the nature of the occasion which calls for the law's interference—the principle being that the law must not undertake more, nor proceed further, than is required for the remedy of the evil or the removal of the mischief.[36]

The same kind of statement is frequently made in the documents with reference to intervention in the life of local communities, cultural groups, churches, labor unions, professional organizations, and other voluntary associations. Not only the government but these other intermediate groups must have power if rights and justice are to be protected.

The problem, of course, is how much power these diverse groups in fact should have and how their activity should be organized and coordinated. The principle of subsidiarity, formally stated, gives priority to the claims of smaller groups and intermediate associations over against the centralizing tendencies of government. The state and other "mega-structures" such as modern corporations are understood as "subsidiary" to the smaller groups. In this the papal statements anticipated Robert Nisbet's thesis that "the major objective of political democracy becomes that of making harmonious and effective the various group allegiances which exist in society, not sterilizing them in the interest of a monistic political community.[37]

At the same time, however, the principle of subsidiarity does justify state intervention whenever this is necessary for the remedy of harm or the promotion of the common good. This legitimacy rests on the classic Roman Catholic distinction between "perfect" and "imperfect" forms of community. The various lower associations in a society, such as the family and different types of voluntary associations are not self-contained and complete in themselves. They are "imperfect societies." The state, however, has as its primary concern the coordination of social life in its totality. Only as political beings are human persons fully social. The state is thus considered a "perfect society," certainly not in the sense that every state is without flaws but rather in the sense that only political society has the resources to protect and promote the total social good. Thus the modern papal teachings are in agreement with Sheldon Wolin's defense of the primacy of the "political"—"that art which strives for an integrative form of direction, one that is broader than that supplied by any group or organization . . . that form of knowledge which deals with what is general and integrative to men, a life of common involvements.[38]

The principle of subsidiarity embodies a pluralist model of social interaction. It envisions society as composed of many groups with many different purposes, needs and legitimate claims. At the same time the principle reasserts the reality of a *common* good which is the concern of society as a whole. Society is not simply a disjointed collection of groups but also an interlocking whole. In Pius XII's words, the state should be "the organic and organizing unity of a real people." This other face of the principle of subsidiarity emphasizes communal solidarity as a counterbalance to the disintegrative effect of competing group claims.[39] The principle of subsidiarity, therefore, does not provide an *a priori* answer to the question of rights conflict. It does not assign an absolute priority to the claims of small or intermediate groups. Its concrete implications, as *Rerum Novarum* stated "must be determined by the nature of the occasion."

In practice, the blending of the pluralist and organicist aspects of the Catholic tradition's model of society has taken a number of more specific shapes over the past hundred years. Throughout the major part of this period the two aspects were combined in a way which assumed the possibility of an harmonious reconciliation of competing group claims under the paternal guidance of the state. In this view, conflict (especially class conflict) was downplayed despite the emphasis on pluralism. Since the Council, however, the optimism of this model has been losing its plausability, but no adequate replacement has yet been found. It will be helpful to illustrate these assertions briefly.

In the writings of Leo XIII and Pius XI the organic relation of the many groups in society was understood by drawing an analogy between social organization and traditional family structures. Society's constituent groups all have legitimate needs and claims. Their different functions and abilities must be protected and promoted. But these functions, like the roles of father, mother and children, are not equal. They are *ordered* under the paternal guidance of the state. Further, this order is hierarchical. Though the intrinsic dignity and values of the many individuals and social groups, like the dignity of all family members, are all equal, this equality is subordinated to the requirements of organic harmony on the institutional level. This subordination is more than recognition of differences in function. It legitimates an unequal recognition of claims on the level of institutional power. It legitimates an inequality of instrumental rights for persons and groups. Some are more equal than others. In Leo XIII's view, the organic order of a pluralistic society depended on a hierarchical stratification of personal roles and group power on the institutional level.[40] In his words:

> The inequality of rights and of power proceeds from the very author of nature "from whom all paternity in heaven and on earth is named." But the minds of princes and their subjects are, according to Catholic doctrine and precepts, bound up one with the other in such a manner, by mutual duties and rights, that the thirst for power is restrained and the rational ground of obedience made easy, firm and noble.[41]

The same institutional inequality despite intrinsic equality was affirmed by Pius XI:

> Let those in power, therefore, be convinced that the more faithfully this principle of "subsidiary" function is followed, and a graded hierarchical order exists between the various associations, the greater also will be both social authority and social efficiency. The happier, too, and more prosperous will be the condition of the commonwealth.[42]

The attempt to reconcile pluralism and organicism by means of a hierarchical order under paternal authority reached its most sophisticated form in the "corporatist" social order advocated by Piux XI. It was presented as an alternative both to the Marxist theory which stressed the conflicting claims of classes and to the liberal theory which emphasized the conflicting claims of individuals. The corporatist model of society was the product of the thought of German Catholic thinkers such as Heinrich Pesch and Gustav Gundlach.[43] It is also reminiscent of the model of social integration which Emil Durkheim called "organic solidarity." In Durkheim's words, societies characterized by organic solidarity

> are constituted, not by a repetition of similar, homogeneous segments, but by a system of different organs each of which has a special role and which are themselves formed of differentiated parts. Not only are social elements not of the same nature, but they are not arranged in the same manner. They are not juxtaposed linearly as the rings of an earthworm, nor entwined one with another, but co-ordinated and subordinated one to another around the same central organ which exercises a moderating action over the rest of the organism.[44]

Howard J. Wiarda has provided a succinct description of the corporatist model. It is a

> system of authority and interest representation, derived chiefly (though not exclusively) from Catholic social thought, stressing functional representation, the integration of capital and labor into a vast web of hierarchically ordered, "harmonious," monopolistic and functionally determined units (or *corporations*), and guided and directed by the state.[45]

As a social theory, corporatism makes the supposition that the problem of conflict will be solved by integrating the different kinds of communities and associations ("corporations") into an organically structured social system. In effect, social conflict is to be eliminated by the creation of a functionally differentiated and hierarchically stratified social organism. The whole system is to be held together by the coordinating authority of the state. Such coordination is the help (the "subsidium") provided by government to the lower communities.

In the corporatist model, therefore, the problem of conflict was sublimated rather than resolved. The theory aimed at the maximum recognition of the rights claims of individuals and of communities such as families, occupational groups and neighborhoods. It also aimed at the organic harmony of society as a whole. The price paid for the denial of conflict between the claims of groups was the legitimation of unequal access to public goods and unequal participation in the shaping of public institutions.[46] It produced a legitimation of inequality in the sphere of instrumental rights. Institutional inequality was demanded because the relation between the plural groups in society was thought of as static. Organic harmony was identified with keeping each group in its assigned place within the whole.[47] If all persons would act in accord with their occupational and familial roles, a harmonious and integrated society would result.

Leo XIII and Pius XI's confidence in their ability to identify a harmonious and changeless system of group and role relations was the Achilles heel of their efforts to balance the need for pluralism with the need for communal solidarity in society as a whole. This confidence was in part a reflection of their conviction that society possesses a rational order which can be identified by human intelligence. It was also an expression of a nostalgia for the institutional structures of the medieval guild order, structures which presumed a hierarchy of status and rights. Pius XI viewed the establishment of corporatism as a "restoration" of the values embodied in this order.

From the beginning of modern Catholic social thought, however, a different way of combining pluralism and communal solidarity can be found in the documents. This counter-pressure arose in Leo XIII's reflections on the *economic* situation of the working class of his time. The institutional structures of economic life were obviously not creating an organic harmony of interests between all social groups and classes. The reality of this conflict led Leo XIII to call for the use of governmental authority to vindicate the legitimate claims of the poor, of the working classes and of organized groups of laborers. Here, the role of public juridical power was not simply to harmonize group interaction according to a pre-existent social model. Rather, its function was to guarantee that these social groups had access to sufficient power to make the claims of their human dignity both known and effective. The growth of this emphasis was evident in Pius XI's use of the standard of social justice as the basis of his call for a reorganization of the institutions of economic life and in Pius XII's emphasis on the need for the juridical protection of the claims of human dignity. In Pius XII's view, both economic and political institutions are instruments for the establishment of greater equality.

John XXIII carried this movement even further when he acknowledged that the achievement of equality in the concrete institutional life of society was one of the "new aspects of the social question." *Mater et Magistra* accepted as one of its presuppositions the fact that

> not only do men grow daily more conscious that they are fully endowed with all the rights of the human person, but they strive mightily that relations among themselves become more equitable and more conformed to human dignity.[48]

Pacem in Terris took an affirmative stance toward the growing insistence that human dignity is violated by economic, sexual, racial and colonial institutions which grant personal privilege by identifying personal worth with some partial role or power.[49] The legitimate claims of persons are not to be identified by specifying their place within a stratified system of statuses and group roles. *Gaudium et Spes* saw the institutionalization of fundamental equality as an urgent task:

> With respect to the fundamental rights of the person, every type of discrimination, whether based on sex, race, color, social condition, language, or religion, is to be eradicated as contrary to God's intent.[50]

Further, the most recent documents of the tradition make very strong judgments about the necessity of positive action to bring about this social equality. It is no longer presumed that personal dignity will be protected by the preservation of existing structures of society, existing social roles, or the existing relationships between economic, cultural, political, religious and familial communities. These are all in need of development.

The balance between pluralism and communal solidarity which is present in the most recent statements assumes that personal dignity is abused by institutionalized inequality of rights. The diversity of functions in society is still clearly recognized, as is the differentiation of communal life into many forms of human association. But no pre-established ordering of the claims of family, cultural and ethnic groups, local communities, occupational groups, the economy as a whole and the state is taken for granted. This order is itself regarded as instrumental and developing.[51] Its function is to guarantee that all persons are enabled to participate actively in those forms of association (including the political) which are necessary for the protection of the claims of their human dignity. Though the recent documents are reluctant to admit the fact, their new orientation implies that communal solidarity is a reality achieved in the midst of social conflict. The balance between pluralism and community is not static but dynamic. It is not organic but conflictual.

An acceptance of a social model which envisions conflict and community as dynamically interrelated would be a major source for the renewal of the Roman Catholic approach to the implementation of human rights. In such a model the large juridical institutions of society would continue to be the chief instruments of communal solidarity. These institutions are "political" in Sheldon Wolin's sense of the term—i.e., they form "an order whose function it would be to integrate the discontinuities of group and organizational life into a common society." [52] Or as Paul VI put it, "As a social being man builds his destiny within a series of groupings which demand, as their completion and as the necessary condition for their development, a vaster society, one of a universal character, the political society." [53] The process of integration of group life does not occur by eliminating either pluralism or conflict. It is rather by recognizing both the positive and negative impacts of these political institutions on the plural groups of society that norms for their organization must be developed. When the "discontinuities of group life" become so great that some groups are denied access to or participation in the economic and political life of the whole community injustice is being done and human rights are being violated. Conversely the same can be said when power is so distributed that one or another privileged group is able to manipulate large economic and political institutions at will. Each of these situations indicates a breakdown of the political order itself. Again in Wolin's words, the effect of such situations "is to deprive citizenship of its meaning and to render political loyalty impossible." [54]

The task of balancing the pluralism of group life with concern for the communal solidarity of society as a whole is thus a task of maintaining a structure of political responsibility and assuring that this responsibility can be exercised by all persons, all groups and society as a whole. Political responsibility is a kind of loyalty to the whole which does not eliminate pluralism or group conflict.

The function of this responsibility is not to create what Nisbet calls a "monistic political community." Rather, political responsibility moderates the disintegrative effects of a group pluralism which is left unchecked by the notion of citizenship. Political responsibility is due to persons and groups *by right*. The large "megastructures" of both government and the economy must be so constructed that all are able to exercise this responsibility. It also includes genuine duties. The maintenance of the political order entails legitimate limitations on the exercise of privileged power, again in both the economic and governmental spheres.

The process of balancing these diverse factors in the political arena is a continual one. There is no *abstract* set of structural norms which determine which groups or which rights claims take priority in a given social and historical moment. This is the implication of Paul VI's statement that Christian social ethics is no longer in a position to propose detailed, normative models of social organization. The principle of subsidiarity, stripped of the hierarchical and corporatist presuppositions which were attached to it in past years, continues to stress the importance of the claims of small and intermediate associations. The need for communal solidarity continues to call for integration of these associations in service of the common good. The developing Catholic model of social interaction is thus fundamentally a set of norms for discerning how these competing and conflicting claims are to be balanced. It is a method for ongoing exercise of political responsibility throughout the whole society. This responsibility falls on all individuals, groups and classes because of their obligations to and claims on society as a whole.

By analogy with Durkheim's notion of organic solidarity, this renewed model of social interaction can be called *political solidarity*. It is a form of social organization which demands participation in and loyalty to the life of society as a whole. It is a form of solidarity which reaches beyond family or vocational group or class. At the same time, it is political rather than organic, for it recognizes that genuine participation of all persons and groups in the common good does not occur in a non-conflictual way. Those competing claims of persons and groups which further greater equality of access to and participation in the common life of society give concrete content to the notion of political solidarity.

Such a normative model of social organization is implicit in the most recent developments of the Catholic rights theory. The future development of the theory will depend on a further explicitation of the normative content of political solidarity. Greater concrete realization of its implications will call for action in the midst of conflict. It will call for political decision. Such advances in both theoretical clarity and in effective realization will depend on historical discernment, a discernment informed by the concrete knowledge that comes from love. In the next section the possible contribution of that form of knowledge to a renewed rights theory will be explored.

Love, Justice and Human Rights

From this analysis it is clear that the principles of justice and the normative model of political solidarity provide guidance and direction for addressing the problem of conflicting claims but do not indicate univocal concrete conclusions. These principles lack that specific content which can only be provided by attention to the particular, detailed and concrete realities of the social situation. As determinants of the structure of the emerging Catholic social ethic, the principles of justice and political solidarity are indispensable tools for the determination of what ought to be done about conflicting claims in particular instances of personal and social decisions. Moral obligation, however, is not primarily an obligation to remain faithful to general principles. Rather, it is a summons to respond affirmatively to the concrete dignity of human persons. Obligation is only concrete, which is to say, obligation only exists at all when it is obligation to protect and promote the dignity and worth of actual human beings.

Though it is clear the tradition is convinced that knowledge of general principles and critical understanding of social patterns have a crucial role to play in concrete moral decision, actual conscientious response to the dignity of human beings is more properly seen as an act of love than as an act of knowledge. In the words of Vatican II, conscience summons moral agents "to love good." It "reveals that law which is fulfilled by love of God and neighbor." [55] It is in love and the deeds of love, rather than in critical reflection, that one acknowledges and affirms the existential worth of another human being or group of human beings.

Critical knowledge—the source of moral principles—reveals different aspects, dimensions and interrelationships of persons. But without the response of love to that concrete call of personal dignity the moral life would not exist at all. We would have only ethics—a set of principles of somewhat indeterminate content, suspended somewhere above the circumstances and particularities of actual human life.[56]

Thus the theory of rights and justice will necessarily remain general and incomplete unless its roots in the experience of love can be shown. Before we are able to draw conclusions about the renewal of the way the tradition seeks to resolve conflicts of claims we must explore the question of how it understands the relationship between rights, justice and love.[57] The development of the understanding of this relationship in modern Catholic teaching has closely paralleled the theological developments traced in the previous chapter. Since Vatican II the official documents show evidence of a loss of full confidence in a single or univocal method of rational thought by which the nature of the human person might be critically understood. The increased awareness of intellectual and social pluralism has been accompanied by a much more explicit reliance on the contribution of theological doctrines and religious belief to the understanding of human dignity. The central biblical injunctions to love God and one's neighbor, to love one's enemies and to have special concern for the poor, the orphan and the widow have assumed a much more central role in recent teachings. The same is true of the teaching and example of Jesus, of the New Testament's central message of Jesus' love "unto death" and of the victory of God's love in the resurrection. These norms are put forward as distinctive Christian contributions in a pluralistic world. Similarly, new awareness of conflict has produced both a decreased confidence that the general principles of justice can provide univocal solutions to conflicts and an increasing number of appeals to a love which is directed to concrete persons in concrete action. A brief examination of the trajectory of these developments reveals much about the developing shape of tradition's approach to conflict. It will also help to further specify the meaning of political solidarity.

Leo XIII's understanding of the relationship between love and justice was of a piece with his conception of the relationship between faith and reason. He did not assert the identity of reason and faith, but rather their perfect fit with each other. As a result, his writings concluded that the concrete claims of human dignity experienced in Christian love or charity can, under ordinary circumstances, be identified with the demands of rights and justice. In Leo's view, Christian love, modeled on the example and teaching of Jesus Christ, is a source of social "concord" and harmony. To the extent that this love is embodied in the lives of citizens, to that extent will social conflict be overcome, rich and poor "will join hands in friendly concord" and "strife must quickly cease." [58] This concord, however was envisioned as a harmony occurring within the framework of Leo XIII's organic conception of social order. For Leo, love creates mutuality and concord within the framework of this social order and assures that the dignity of all is respected in the midst of social stratification. At the same time, however, the acceptance of a stratified social order limits the claims of love in society. The demands of love, in the social sphere, did not challenge the basic structures of social relationships which Leo XIII took for granted.[59] Such a challenge is unnecessary, Leo XIII implied, because these structures both can and do support the dignity of all persons provided they are not strained by immoderate self-assertion.

Leo admitted that love may sometimes call for action which goes beyond the forms of behavior expected in a society so organized, especially when a person or group is attempting to heal the consequences of previous injustices. But the hierarchic model of a just social order and the demands of love are mutually determining even in this limited case:

> True, no one is commanded to distribute to others that which is required for his own needs and those of his household; nor even to give away what is reasonably required to keep up becomingly his condition in life, "for no one ought to live other than becomingly." But, when what necessity demands has been supplied and one's standing fairly been taken thought for, it becomes a duty to give to the indigent what remains over.[60]

Thus in Leo XIII we see a very high degree of confidence that reasoned reflection on the nature of the person in society can reach the same degree of concreteness as can the experience of love and the call of conscience. This is so largely because of Leo's confidence that he knew what the distribution of roles and authority in society should look like. His affirmation of the concord between love and justice resulted from his belief that demands of justice and rights were unchanging. Reason could know them in detail. The social implications of Chrisitan love could be captured and expressed in the principles of justice and embodied in a stratified organic social order.

The great value of this model was its insistence that Christian love could not be genuine unless it led to just action. However, it kept the full power of the biblical call for love of neighbor and the prophetic challenge of the teaching and life of Jesus within the narrow boundaries of limited conception of social order and organic harmony. The religious perspective which could have led to a quite different method of adjudicating conflicting claims was narrowed by the philosophical and social models employed. Such an approach to the relation between love and justice was doomed to be overthrown by the recognition of the inadequacy of the hierarchic model, by the increasing recognition of the historical development of social structures and by the awareness of intellectual and social pluralism which emerged at Vatican II.

The same confidence in the substantive harmony of the call of love and the demands of justice was stated explicitly in the writings of Pius XI and Pius XII. Pius XI did not see justice and love primarily as supplementary to each other but rather as different ways of expressing a single obligation:

> Charity will never be true charity unless it takes justice into account. The Apostle teaches that "he who loveth his neighbor has fulfilled the law," and he gives the reason: "For, thou shalt not commit adultery, thou shalt not kill, thou shalt not steal . . . and if there be any other commandment, it is summed up in this saying, 'Thou shalt love thy neighbor as thyself' " (Rom 13:8-9). According to the Apostle, then, all the commandments, including those which are of strict justice as those which forbid us to kill or to steal, may be re-

> duced to the single precept of true charity. From this it follows that a "charity" which deprives the workingman of the salary to which he has a strict title in justice is not charity at all, but only its empty name and semblance. The wage earner is not to receive as alms what is his due in justice. And let no one attempt with trifling charitable donation to exempt himself from the great duties imposed by justice. Both justice and charity often dictate obligations touching on the same subject but under different aspects.[61]

In this passage, and many others like it, Pius XI sets the meaning of genuine love by an appeal to the principles of justice.

Justice and love were portrayed by Pius XI and Pius XII as related to each other as matter and form, as body and soul.[62] Justice describes the structured content of the mutual respect for dignity in society. Charity is the life of that structure, the experience in which mutual union is realized. Pius XI quotes St. Thomas in support of this view:

> True and authentic peace emanates from charity rather than from justice, since justice merely removes the obstacles to peace, such as wrongs and injuries, whereas peace is peculiarly and properly the object of charity.[63]

This same organic conception of the relationship between the principles of justice and the call of love was upheld by Pius XII:

> On this organic conception which alone is living, in which the noblest humanity and the most genuine Christian spirit flourish in harmony, there is marked the Scripture thought, expounded by the great Aquinas: *Opus Justitiae Pax*—The work of justice shall be peace—a thought which is applicable to the internal as to the external aspect of social life. It admits of neither contrast nor alternative such as expressed in the disjunction, love or right, but the fruitful synthesis of love and right. In the one as in the other, since both radiate from the same spirit of God, we read the program and the seal of the human spirit; they complement one another, give each

> other life and support, walk hand in hand along the road of concord and pacification, while right clears the way for love and love makes right less stern and gives it higher meaning. Both elevate human life to that social atmosphere where even amid the failings, the obstacles and the difficulties of the earth a fraternal community of life is made possible.[64]

The same relative confidence in the ability to capture the demands of love in the principles of justice which was present in Leo XIII continued in Pius XI and Pius XII. The loving response to concrete persons produces a form of communal solidarity whose shape is organic and conflict-free—"*opus justitiae pax*."

The gradual loss of a firm conception of the organic order in a stratified society was not without its effect on the conception of the love/justice relation, however. This breakdown of the early Leonine conception of social order reached its conclusion with the recognition of the importance of social context and historicity in John XXIII and Vatican II. This transition led to the recognition that love and the response of conscience to the concrete call of human dignity can precede the ability of reason to formulate moral obligation in precise moral principles. This shift coincided with Vatican II's recognition that the pluralism of rational methodologies calls for a much more explicit reliance on theological doctrines and religious symbols in the attempt to describe the nature of the human person. The Conciliar breakthrough also called for a recognition of the fact that the call to love in action extends further than the limits of organic harmony. Indeed, the obligation to love can be a call to engage in conflict. The result of these transitions has been a markedly new emphasis on the importance of love and the centrality of a conscience shaped by the symbols of Christian faith for the discernment of the demands of social morality.

The developments accompanying Vatican II reached their fullest expression in Paul VI's *Octogesima Adveniens* and the 1971 Synod document, Justice in the World. *Octogesima Adveniens* is positive but critical in its evaluation of the adequacy of both the human sciences and of all societal models. Consequently, it hesitates to claim that a detailed rational scheme or ideology can determine precisely what form of social action is called for in the concrete.[65] The principles of justice continue to be operative in forming the judgments of the Christian. These principles, however, cannot be used to determine in detail the "models of society" which are most in harmony with the dignity of the human person.[66] Rather, Paul VI maintains, an "ever finer discernment" based on a "transcendent love for man" is needed "to strike at the roots of injustice and to establish a justice which will be less and less imperfect." [67] The priority here is clearly on love. Love for concrete persons in society is the source of development of the social ethic of Catholicism according to the recent view. The principles of justice remain as guidelines and norms. They remain principles of discernment guiding prudential decisions. But, concrete love for persons—both as individuals and as members of society—is the only pathway to the discovery of the concrete meaning of justice and rights in a given social-political situation. The Conciliar documents once again raise the question of whether the tradition of reasoned reflection as the basis of moral action is able to withstand the relativizing tendencies of modern historical consciousness. In abandoning the neo-scholastic confidence that reason can know the content of social-moral obligation in detail, it might appear that recent Catholic thought has set aside all hope of establishing priorities among competing rights claims.

However, this need not be the case if the tradition continues to develop among the trajectory we have been tracing. For when the post-Conciliar documents are viewed as a whole it is clear that the appeal to love is not without content. Love is neither a vague emotion compatible with any and every approach to conflicting claims. Neither is it simply a motive capable of putting the energy of personal or group action behind any one of the many human rights policies being proposed in contemporary debate. In analyzing the way appeals to love are made in the concrete discussions of rights policy in the recent documents it can be seen to correspond to the normative standard of political solidarity proposed in the previous section. By clarifying what the documents see as *concrete* demands of love in the present historical moment the meaning of political responsibility in the midst of conflict will be illuminated. Such a clarification will provide a basis for the renewal of the Catholic rights theory which this book envisions.

IN QUEST OF POLITICAL SOLIDARITY

A love shaped by Christian faith has a two-fold content that can provide guidance in the difficult task of establishing priorities between conflicting claims. First, love is response to persons in their uniqueness and individuality. The appeal to love as a standard of social morality means that an adequate theory of human rights cannot be based on a formal or abstract understanding of what respect for human dignity demands. The many philosophical and social scientific analyses of the nature of social existence are indispensable in the effort to develop a theory of human rights and a policy for the protection of rights. But unless such theories and policies are rooted in attention to the unique social situations, potentialities and needs of persons they will finally subordinate people to ideology. As Paul VI put it:

> If, beyond legal rules, there is really no deeper feeling of respect for and service to others, then even equality before the law can serve as an alibi for flagrant discrimination, continued exploitation and actual contempt.[68]

This "deeper feeling of respect" takes into account not just the similarities between persons but also their differences. It provides the basis for a human rights policy which grants priority to the claims of those whose human dignity is especially threatened by the concrete circumstances of their lives. In a social world which is developing and constantly assuming new organizational patterns, the particularity of the response of love reveals areas where human dignity is newly threatened or presently unprotected. It shows which persons need increased social and institutional protection. It grants priority to the claims of these persons and establishes "preference rules" for an adequate human rights policy.

Thus, since Vatican II, the documents have emphasized the

importance of discriminating (or discerning) attention to the differences in the way social institutions affect the dignity of different groups and classes of persons. Specifically, such attention means granting special priority to meeting minimum human needs for food, clothing, shelter and other basic necessities of human life. The economic patterns of contemporary society, especially in the international domain, have created an enormous inequality in levels of nutrition, health, housing and basic social services. Staggeringly large numbers of persons live well below the human minimum in these basic areas. In the recent documents, as in the earlier phases of the tradition, claims to the fulfillment of these needs are not granted theoretical priority over claims to civil and political liberty. Both bread and freedom are essential to human dignity. But love and its attention to the concrete grants priority to claims arising from need in a practical human rights policy. When conflicts arise between the claims of the poor and those of the rich or between the claims of the economically powerful and the socially marginal, discerning love grants priority to the claims of those in need over those who are well off. In other words, persons in need have a *right* to have the minimum human standard met in their own case before the less basic desires and aspirations of others are fulfilled. As *Populorum Progressio* put it, quoting St. John and St. Ambrose:

> "He who has the goods of this world and sees his brother in need and closes his heart to him, how does the love of God abide in him?" It is well known to all how seriously the Fathers of the Church described the obligation of the affluent to those in need: "You are not making a gift to the poor man from your possessions" says St. Ambrose, "but you are returning what is his." . . . No one is allowed to set aside solely for his own advantage possessions which exceed his needs when others lack the necessities of life.[69]

Therefore, in an affluent society especially, claims based on need deserve to be granted priority status in a human rights policy. This is the response of a community which embodies political solidarity when some of its members are in need.[70]

There is a second dimension of the content of love which provides additional guidance in establishing priorities for a human rights policy and in concretizing the meaning of political solidarity. Stress on the claims of material need is not the only contribution which the new emphasis on love has made in the recent documents. The experience of love not only entails an affirmation of the concrete reality and worth of other persons but also leads to union between persons, for example, the interpersonal communion of friendship and the solidarity of various social and political groups. The experience of love reveals that the realization of human dignity occurs only through the formation of bonds with other persons and groups. In the present historical moment the strengthening of these bonds is an especially urgent task if large groups of persons are not to be degraded and excluded from active participation in the common good. In the view of Vatican II, "solidarity in action at this turning point in history is a matter of urgency."[71] In even stronger language, the Synod document on Justice in the World sees in the present situation a "crisis of universal solidarity." [72] Though perhaps not as intense as interpersonal communion, the experience of social love or communal solidarity is regarded by the recent documents as another source of knowledge of the priorities which ought to be set for conflicting claims. Thus the priorities of a human rights policy must be formulated within the context of the affective affirmation of human interdependence which is the basis for solidarity.

The recent documents do not call for unlimited self-sacrifice in the interest of the good of others, nor do they subordinate rights to the good of the whole in a totalitarian sense. The demands of solidarity do, however, imply a *preference* for limiting claims to individual or group autonomy in the interest of social union when such autonomy is leading to the exclusion of some from the political, economic or cultural life of society. In the words of *Octogesima Adveniens,* when this dimension of love is made active in society

> human groups will gradually begin to share and to live as communities. Thus freedom, which too often asserts itself as a claim for autonomy by opposing the freedom of others, will

> develop in its deepest human reality: to involve itself and spend itself in building up active and lived solidarity.[73]

In this passage, the claims of freedom are not denied or even minimized. Neither is the reality of conflict denied. Rather, freedom is interpreted as a form of participation in social life. Conflict is moderated and channeled by the obligations of citizenship and the political order. The patterns of present social life make access to the public goods of the economic and political spheres an extremely urgent matter for large numbers of persons. Because this is so the documents are willing to grant this kind of participatory freedom a priority over the freedom of powerful persons or groups to act autonomously in their own interest whether in the economic or governmental spheres. This priority gives specific content to the notion of political solidarity and indicates in a general way how it should be applied to the competing claims of different social groups. It suggests that the power of government intervention can be legitimately used to support the claims to economic and political participation which are made by groups who are presently denied to these public goods. Government intervention may be used to limit the exercise of economic and political power by groups whose present disproportionate share excludes others.

From this analysis of the developing approach to rights conflict we can draw several conclusions. First, the tradition does possess several important principles which are important in sorting out conflicting claims. The tripartite principle of justice and the principle of subsidiarity insure that the nature of these conflicts is viewed in its full complexity. Commutative, distributive and social justice demand that both the private and public dimensions of these conflicts be taken into account in formulating a human rights policy. The principle of subsidiarity points out that persons are members of many different kinds of communities. They thus have rightful claims to both freedom and participation in as many different social spheres or sectors. Neither of these two principles, however, establishes concrete priorities for a human rights policy. This is a task of historical discernment, love and political solidarity.

Because all the social models which have been and are being used to establish priorities are incomplete descriptions of the full richness of human community, a more concrete form of knowledge is needed for the establishment of these priorities. The recent tradition appeals the experience of love as the source of such knowledge. Love as affirmative response to concrete persons, especially those in need, and love as solidarity and co-participation with others, are the context for the ordering of competing claims. This order grants priority to the claims of human need over the claims of unlimited personal desire. It grants priority to the participation of those who are presently excluded from public goods over the unrestrained freedom and use of power by those whose actions are the cause of this exclusion. In the final chapter of this book these preference rules and concrete priorities will be examined in greater detail. They are the key to the present and future shape of the Roman Catholic approach to human rights.

One final note about the specifically religious aspects of these priorities is in order. It is clear that not all will agree with the priorities sketched in outline here. The post-Conciliar acknowledgement of intellectual and social pluralism is consistent with this disagreement. The fact of pluralism, however, should not prevent the Roman Catholic Church from offering these priorities as interpretations of the demands of human dignity in our time. Neither should it prevent the Catholic Church from increased institutional action to insure the implementation of these priorities. As one among many voices in the human rights debate, the Catholic Church can legitimately propose these priorities for public acceptance. Such proposals are themselves an exercise of political solidarity. They are attempts to insure the maintainence and improvement of the political order itself, in both its governmental and economic dimensions.

The final chapter of this book will interpret these proposals more systematically and in greater detail. Their practical usefulness and systematic cogency are the test of their claim to normative universality.

NOTES

1. *JW,* no. 15.

2. It is significant in this regard that rights language is notably deemphasized in the various forms of liberation theology recently developed within Roman Catholicism, forms of theology which place heavy emphasis on the reality of social conflict. For example, there is no entry for "human rights" or even "human dignity" in the extensive index of Gustavo Gutierrez' *A Theology of Liberation,* trans. S. Caridad Inda and John Eagleson (Maryknoll, N.Y.: Orbis, 1973). One explanation of the abandonment of rights language lies in the fact that that language is linked with static and individualistic notions of the human person in the minds of these theologians. See Juan Luis Segundo, S.J., *The Community Called Church,* vol. 1 of *A Theology for Artisans of a New Humanity,* trans. John Drury (Maryknoll, N.Y.: Orbis, 1973), esp. pp. 128-132.

3. The phrase is Reinhold Niebuhr's. See *The Nature and Destiny of Man,* vol. 2, p. 72. Though Niebuhr's understanding of justice is notably different from that found in the Catholic tradition, both address the problem of competing claims.

4. *RN,* nos. 1 and 2. See *GC,* no. 1.

5. Though the parallel is not perfect, the distinction being drawn here between rights and justice is similar to the frequently debated question of the relation between rights and duties.

6. For example, *Pacem in Terris* declares that all the rights it enumerates are part of an *order* which "the Creator of the world has imprinted in man's heart" and by which "men are most admirably taught, first of all how they should conduct their mutual dealings among themselves, then how the relationships between the citizens and the public authorities of each State should be regulated, then how States should deal with one another, and finally how, on the one hand individual men and States, and on the other hand the community of all peoples should act towards each other, the establishment of such a community being urgently demanded today by the requirements of the universal common good." *PT,* nos. 5 and 7. The notion of an *order* of rights, prevalent throughout the tradition, and especially emphasized since Pius XII, reveals the relational character of all rights. From this perspective it is clear that *a* right or any given set of single rights is not to be conceived of as the atomic building blocks of the moral universe. The repeated correlation of rights and duties brings this point home. See *PT,* nos. 28-34.

7. See, e.g., *QA,* no. 58.

8. These three modalities of justice were, of course, not the invention of the modern papal tradition. The distinction between commutative justice and distributive justice has Aristotelian roots (see *Nicomachean Ethics,* 1131a-1134b). The tripartite division entered the modern Catholic tradition from a reconsideration of several passages from Thomas

Aquinas, esp. *Summa Theologiae,* IIa-IIae, q. 58, art. 2, 5 and 6 and q. 61, art. 1-3. Analysis of these passages can be found in Thomas Gilby, *Between Community and Society: A Philosophy and Theology of the State,* (London: Longmans, Green and Co., 1953), pp. 208-213. Calvez and Perrin trace the history of the controversy surrounding the meaning of St. Thomas's division of justice which raged among the "social Catholics" in the late nineteenth and early twentieth centuries. *The Church and Social Justice,* Chap. VI, "Justice." For an early interpretation and application of these texts which ultimately became official teaching in Pius XI see Charles Antoine, *Cours d'economie sociale,* 4th ed. (Paris: Felix Alcan, 1908), Chap. V, "Justice et Charité." The debate was also carried on among the authors of the moral manuals. A good summary from within the manualist tradition can be found in Marcellino Zalba, S.J., *Theologiae Moralis Summa,* vol. II, (Madrid: Biblioteca de Autores Cristianos, 1953), pp. 453-461. The interpretation of the papal discussions of justice presented in this chapter is in the main supported by these authors.

9. For an elaboration on these definitions see, for example, E. Genicot, S.J., *Institutiones Theologiae Moralis,* (Bruges: Desclée de Brouwer, 1951), pp. 393–394. The contrast between distributive and aggregative principles of social morality is developed in a different but illuminating way by Brian Barry in his book *Political Argument* (London: Routledge & Kegan Paul, 1965), esp. pp. 43–44.

10. *QA,* no. 110.

11. *Nicomachean Ethics,* 1132a. See also, St. Thomas Aquinas, *Summa Theologiae,* IIa-IIae, q. 61, art. 2 and Johannes Messner, *Social Ethics: Natural Law in the Modern World,* trans. J. J. Doherty (St. Louis: B. Herder Book Co., 1957), p. 219. It is important to note that equality between labor and wages is not determined solely by a formal equality of consent in the wage contract. See *RN,* no. 44.

12. See Arthurus Vermeersch, *Theologiae Moralis,* (Roma: Universita Gregoriana, 1928), vol. II, pp. 305-306.

13. Douglas Sturm,"On Meanings of Public Good: An Exploration," *Journal of Religion* 58 (1978), p. 23.

14. *RN,* no. 33. The citation is from the *Summa Theologiae,* IIa-IIae, q. 61, *art.* 1, ad. 2.

15. Leo XIII does not say that all have a right to an equal share, but that all equally have a right to some share of these public goods. See Zalba, *Theologiae Moralis Summa,* II, pp. 445-446. The relation between these two types of equality is discussed in the second section of this chapter.

16. For an excellent treatment of this passage see Thomas Gilby, *Between Community and Society,* Chap. VIII, "The Concept of a Group," esp. pp. 105-106.

17. John A. Ryan has identified six dimensions of distributive justice, which he treats in six "canons" of distributive justice: the canons of equality, need, effort, productivity, scarcity, and total human welfare.

See his *Distributive Justice: The Right and Wrong of Our Present Distribution of Wealth* (New York: Macmillan, 1927), chap. XVI, "The Principal Canons of Distributive Justice." Our reading of the encyclicals produces what is essentially a conflation and simplification of Ryan's conclusions. It is an unfortunate symptom of the tendency of contemporary philosophers to ignore the ethical thought developed within religious traditions that Nicholas Rescher has felt free to borrow this chapter of Ryan's book with relatively minor alterations in his recent treatment of the subject. In *Distributive Justice* (Indianapolis: Bobbs Merrill, 1966), Rescher essentially summarizes Ryan's position (Chap. 4, "The Canons of Distributive Justice and the Foundation of Claims") with the rather understated acknowledgement that the material has been "competently and instructively discussed" by Ryan.

18. *QA,* no. 60. This understanding is present throughout the tradition. For example, John XXIII reaffirmed it: "The very nature of the common good requires that all members of the state be entitled to share in it although in different ways according to each one's task, merits, and circumstances. For this reason, every civil authority must take pains to promote the common good of all, without preference for any single citizen or civic group." *PT,* no. 56.

19. *QA,* nos. 69 and 71.

20. *RN,* no. 44. See *RN,* nos. 6 and 7.

21. *QA,* no. 53; *MM,* nos. 74-76.

22. See Ryan, *Distributive Justice,* chap. XVI.

23. Arthur F. Utz states the point nicely by drawing a distinction between this type of rights theory and that which sees all rights as essentially private: "Während im positiven Rechtsdenken das subjective öffentliche Recht einen Anspruch gegen die Gemeinschaft besagt, also geradezu individualistisch subjectives Recht im Sinne der Verkehrsgerechtigkeit (justitia commutativa) ist, kann im Naturrecht das sogen. subjective Recht nur immer ein personales Recht im Rahmen des Ganzen sein." *Formen und Grenzen des Subsidiaritätsprinzips* (Heidelberg: F. H. Kerle Verlag, 1956), p. 25.

24. *DR,* no. 52.

25. *QA,* no. 88.

26. Nell-Breuning, *Reorganization,* pp. 249-50.

27. See *QA,* nos. 51, 57, 58, 110; *DR,* no. 52; *SP,* no. 54; *MM,* nos. 71-73.

28. See *DR,* nos. 52 and 53; *MM,* nos. 71-73 and 79-81; *PT,* no. 64.

29. John Rawls, *A Theory of Justice,* pp. 9-10.

30. See Peter L. Berger and Richard John Neuhaus *To Empower People: The Role of Mediating Structures in Public Policy* (Washington, D.C.: American Enterprise Institute, 1977), p. 2.

31. For two different perspectives on these disagreements and the central role they play in contemporary social and political theory, see Robert A. Nisbet, *The Quest for Community* (New York: Oxford University Press, 1973) esp. Chap. 11, and Sheldon S. Wolin, *Politics and Vi-*

sion: Continuity and Innovation in Western Political Thought (Boston: Little, Brown, 1960), Chap. 10.

32. *QA,* no. 79. A considerable body of Catholic literature exists on this principle. The treatment which follows is dependent on the writings listed here, even though it departs from all of them to a greater or lesser degree: Messner, *Social Ethics,* Pt. III, "The Order of Society," esp. pp. 192-200; 436-446; Richard E. Mulcahy, S.J., "Subsidiarity," *New Catholic Encyclopedia,* vol. 13, pp. 762-63; Nell-Breuning, *Reorganization,* Chap. X, "The New Social Order," esp. pp. 205–09; idem, "Zur Sozialreform, Erwägungen zum Subsidiaritätsprinzip," *Stimmen der Zeit* 157. Bd. 81, (1955/56), pp. 1-11; Arthur-Fridolin Utz, *Formen und Grenzen des Subsidiaritätsprinzips;* idem, *Grundsätze der Socialpolitik;* H. Weber, "Solidarität," *Die Religion in Geschichte und Gegenwart,* 3rd rev. ed., vol. 6, pp. 130–31; idem, "Subsidiarität," *Die Religion in Geschichte und Gegenwart,* 3rd rev. ed., vol. 6, p. 455. Unfortunately, Andrew Greeley, whose passionate interpretation of the principle is set forth in his *No Bigger than Necessary,* does not seem to be aware of the important contributions made by German Catholic thinkers, especially Utz and Nell-Breuning.

33. Roberto Mangabeira Unger, *Knowledge and Politics* (New York: Free Press, 1975), p. 74.

34. Christmas Address 1944, in Yzermans, II, p. 81. See Christmas Address 1952, in Yzermans, II, pp. 163, 171–172 and Christmas Address 1951, in Yzermans, II, p. 156. An excellent analysis of the Thomistic and scholastic views which lie behind these texts can be found in Gilby, *Between Community and Society,* chaps. VI and VII.

35. Michael Walzer has developed a similar argument, probably unaware of the parallel between his thought and the Catholic tradition, in his *Obligations: Reflections on Disobedience, War and Citizenship* (New York: Simon and Schuster, 1970), chap. 10, "The Problem of Citizenship." James Rausch has pointed out this parallel in "Dignitatis Humanae: The Unfinished Agenda," in W. J. Burghardt, ed., *Religious Liberty: 1965-1975,* (New York: Paulist Press, 1976), p. 46.

36. *RN,* nos. 35-36. Similar statements can be found in *RN,* nos. 32, 47, and 50.

37. Robert A. Nisbet, *The Quest for Community,* p. 250.

38. Sheldon S. Wolin, *Politics and Vision,* p. 434.

39. See Weber, "Subsidiarität," p. 455.

40. James Hennesey, S.J., has pointed out the continuity between Leo XIII and that bulwark of medieval intellectual and social order, Pius IX, in "Leo XIII's Thomistic Revival: A Political and Philosophical Event," *Journal of Religion,* 58 (1978), Supplement, pp. S185–97.

41. *QAM,* no. 5. This view is found throughout the writings of Leo XIII. See *AP,* no. 29, *Inscrut,* no. 1, *Diut,* nos. 4, 11 and 16, *HG,* nos. 1-, 22, *ID,* nos. 3, 4 and 18, *IP,* no. 8, *Lib,* nos. 9 and 13. See Murray, "Leo XIII: Two Concepts of Government, II."

42. *QA,* no. 80.

43. See, for example, Richard E. Mulcahy, S.J., *The Economics of Henrich Pesch* (New York: Holt, 1952) and Gustav Gundlach, S.J., "Solidarismus," *Staatslexicon,* 5th ed. (1931), Bd. 4, 1613-1621.

44. Emil Durkheim, *On Morality and Society,* ed. Robert N. Bellah (Chicago: University of Chicago Press, 1973). Durkheim's advocacy of a social order structured around occupational groups is also echoed in Pius XI.

45. "Corporatism and Development in the Iberic-Latin World: Persistent Strains and New Variations," *Review of Politics* 36 (1974), p. 6. This entire issue of the *Review of Politics* is devoted to a reevaluation and reexamination of corporatism in the light of its contemporary resurgence in Latin America. Unger's description of this social theory is similar to Wiarda's: "Conservative corporatism seeks to resolve the conflicts of the liberal state and of the bureaucratic institution by restoring an idealized version of the principle of estates. It looks to the corporate bodies of preliberal society as models for the ideal community. The social order is to consist of a hierarchy of groups, each represented in higher level associations and ultimately in a central government." *Knowledge and Politics,* p. 249.

46. *DR,* nos. 31-33. See Nell-Breuning, *Reorganization,* p. 206, no. 3.

47. See Unger, *Knowledge and Politics,* p. 250. For a collection of provocative studies of the links between the corporatist legacy and the resurgence of authoritarian regimes in recent years see James M. Malloy, ed., *Authoritarianism and Corporatism in Latin America,* (Pittsburgh: University of Pittsburgh Press, 1977).

48. *MM,* no. 211. See nos. 71-74, 135, 140 and 168; *QA,* no. 22 and *JW,* no. 7.

49. *PT,* nos. 39-45, 48, 56, 63, 86, 89 and 125.

50. *GS,* no. 29. See nos. 7, 8, 63, 64 and 66.

51. See Utz, *Formen und Grenzen der Subsidiaritätsprinzips,* pp. 74 and 78.

52. Sheldon Wolin, *Politics and Vision,* p. 432.

53. *OA,* no. 24. See *GS,* no. 74.

54. Sheldon Wolin, *Politics and Vision,* p. 433.

55. *GS,* no. 16.

56. For an excellent discussion of the relationship of conscience and principle which represents the best of the Roman Catholic tradition on this point, see Karl Rahner's well known essay, "On the Question of a Formal Existential Ethics," *Theological Investigations,* vol. II, pp. 235-64. Edward Schillebeeckx makes the point we are discussing here most forcefully in his provocative essay, "The Magisterium and the World of Politics," in J. Metz, ed., *Faith and the World of Politics, Concilium,* no. 36 (New York: Paulist Press, 1968). Schillebeeckx, in line with the best of the tradition, objects to the notion that concrete obligation can be de-

duced from general principles. Rather, general principles which highlight certain aspects of the genuinely human are formed as a result of concrete experiences of obligation. In Schillebeeckx's words, " 'to be human' is not a part of the real, i.e., individual and concrete, human person *side by side* with another part which would constitute individuality; for the individuality determines 'being human' *from within*. Only and exclusively as intrinsically individualized is 'being human' a reality and can it be the source of moral norms (which in religious parlance we describe as the will of God). Therefore, there is only one source of ethical norms, namely, the *historical reality* of the value of the inviolable human person with all its bodily and social implications. Moreover, no abstract statement can produce a call or invitation" (p. 27). Richard McCormick, S.J. has pointed out the inadequacy of an exclusive reliance on principles formulated by critical reason as the basis of moral obligation despite his conviction that principles are indispensable. The inadequacy of principles, McCormick suggests, is "a reflection of the gap that exists between our moral sensitivities and judgments, and our ability to systematize them rationally. Moral awareness and judgments are fuller and deeper than 'rational arguments' and 'rational categories.' " *Ambiguity in Moral Choice,* The 1973 Pere Marquette Theology Lecture (Milwaukee: Marquette University, 1973), p. 106. See Unger, *Knowledge and Politics,* pp. 253-259.

57. The relation of love and justice is one of the most debated points in modern Christian ethics, especially among Protestant thinkers. This treatment cannot and does not aim to provide a systematic survey of the literature on this question. Gene Outka has undertaken such a task in *Agape: An Ethical Analysis,* chap. 3, "Agape and Justice." What follows, however, is shaped in significant ways by these recent discussions. The same can be said about the debates concerning the relationship between principles and situations, rules and deeds, or norms and contexts. On these subjects, in addition to the writings cited in the preceding note, see James M. Gustafson, "Context versus Principles: A Misplaced Debate in Christian Ethics," Paul Ramsey, *Deeds and Rules in Christian Ethics* (New York: Scribner's, 1967), Bruno Schüller, *Die Begründung sittlicher Urteile: Typen ethischer Argumentation in der katholischen Moraltheologie* (Düsseldorf: Patmos Verlag, 1973), and Paul Tillich, *Love, Power and Justice* (New York: Oxford University Press, 1960).

58. *RN,* nos. 24-25.

59. See *RN,* no. 22.

60. *RN,* no. 22. The reference is to St. Thomas, *Summa Theologiae,* IIa-IIae, q. 32, art. 6. For a more thorough analysis of "charity as a palliative" for injustice, see Calvez and Perrin, pp. 165-68. See also *QAM,* no. 9, *GC,* nos. 16 and 20, and *RN,* nos. 30-31.

61. *DR,* no. 50. See *UA,* nos. 2 and 41; *QA,* nos. 3, 88, 126 and 131.

62. *QA,* no. 88.

63. *Summa Theologiae*, IIa-IIae, q. 29, art. 3, ad. 3. This passage is referred to in *UA*, no. 38 and *QA*, no. 137. See Calvez and Perrin, pp. 168-73.

64. Christmas Address 1942, In Yzermans, II, pp. 56–57.

65. *OA*, no. 40.

66. *OA*, no. 40.

67. *OA*, nos. 15 and 45. See *OA*, no. 4.

68. *OA*, no. 23.

69. *PP*, no. 23. The quotations are from 1 John 3:17 and from St. Ambrose, *De Nabuthe*, chap. 12, no. 53 (*PL* 14, 747). See *GS*, no. 69.

70. This kind of development in the tradition would bear out Gene Outka's conclusions about the influence which an agapeic notion of love will have on a theory of social justice: "One issue agape is likely to affect is that of priorities. For agapeistic pressures appear to extend by and large in the following directions: needs typically will be emphasized before merit, other sorts of differences between persons (beyond differential treatment based on different needs) will be played down, and privilege will always have to be justified." *Agape: An Ethical Analysis*, p. 92.

71. *GS*, no. 10. Quoted in *OA*, no. 5. See also *PP*, nos. 48, 64, 73 and 85.

72. *JW*, subtitle of the first section of Part I.

73. *OA*, no. 47.

Chapter Five
Toward Policy

The previous chapter has argued that the chief element in the Catholic rights theory which is in need of renewal is its understanding of social conflict. The community which is the bearer of this tradition is no stranger to the reality of conflict and compromise. It is a community with complex organizational structures and institutional self-interests. It is also a community which is present and visible in nearly all societies around the globe and on all levels of society, from the family to the United Nations. No community of this sort can avoid making decisions about the conflicting claims which appeal for concern and support.[1] The Church has felt these conflicting claims in its efforts to contribute to the protection and promotion of human dignity and will continue to do so. The tradition's normative theory of how conflicts between claims are to be resolved, however, is much less developed than it needs to be. Any human rights theory which lacks a well-articulated approach to conflicts between claims will be forced to deal with conflict in an *ad hoc* and unpredictable way.[2]

The great strength of both the interest-group pluralism of liberal democracy and the state socialism of Marxism-Leninism is the explicitness with which they address both the normative and structural problems of claim conflict. Both theories have generated normative priorities which provide the basis for social strategy and public policy. The Catholic theory has been at pains to avoid the narrowing of the sphere of rights which both of these other traditions have been subject to. As a result the strategic moral priorities of the Catholic rights theory are less developed than are its ultimate foundations. The purpose of this chapter is to elaborate the priorities proposed in the conclusion of the last chapter as both coherent with the tradition and responsive to the actual conflicts of the contemporary world. These priorities do not constitute a human rights policy. They do, however, indicate how the Catholic rights theory can contribute to the formation of policy.

We shall proceed by first reaffirming the tradition's insistence on the importance of protecting rights in all spheres of activity where human dignity is at stake. The establishment of priorities is not a matter of choosing between Marxist and liberal approaches. The protection of the full range of human rights under present social conditions implies a particular ordering of institutional processes and instrumental rights in *both* the economic *and* the political spheres. This ordering we will call a strategic morality. It is strategic because it is formulated from analysis of the kinds of social activity which will lead to the protection of the rightful claims of all persons under present social conditions. It is a morality because it represents a way of responding to the genuine claims of human dignity. The second section of the chapter will argue that the strategic morality suited to the present economic and political situation must give priority to the establishment of social rights for all. Institutional processes and instrumental rights are subordinate to the protection of social rights in each of the three fundamental sectors of need, freedom and relationship. Similarly, the exercise of personal rights is limited by the strategic centrality of social rights. The use of institutional power to limit privilege and enhance participation is the present strategic demand of political solidarity and practical implication of the Catholic human rights tradition. The chapter will conclude by specifying three priority principles for human rights policies which are responsive to these strategic moral demands.

STRATEGIC MORALITY

Our review of the Catholic tradition has repeatedly noted the tradition's emphasis on the importance of the full range of human rights—physical, social, economic, political, religious, familial, cultural etc. In this regard the Catholic theory closely resembles the inclusive approach to human rights adopted in the

U.N. Declaration of Covenants. From a theoretical and normative point of view this inclusiveness is fully justified. Human dignity is indeed at stake in all of these areas. More needs to be said, however, if the theory is to have bearing on practical efforts to institutionalize and implement human rights.

The two most intellectually vigorous ways in which the problems of institutionalization and implementation are currently addressed are derived from the traditions of liberal democracy and Marxism-Leninism. The flaw in both these traditions, as we have argued in Chapter One, is the way they confuse instrumental means for the protection of rights with the foundation and full content of rights. The "lexical" priority of liberty over other basic human goods in liberal thought is the result of a conviction about the capacity of government to promote economic and social rights without undermining personal liberty. The judgment upon which liberal democracy rests its theoretical case for the priority of liberty is in large measure a judgment about the capacity and flexibility of political and economic institutions. Such thinkers as Rawls, Cranston, Berlin and Hart do not deny that food, housing, health care and cultural identity are genuine goods which are essential for a life truly characterized by dignity. Rather, they have reached a strategic judgment on the basis of historical experience that human persons are better served overall if priority is granted to personal liberty and immunity from interference by others.

Similarly, Marxist thought relies on historical 'udgment about the way the distribution of the instruments of power along class lines shapes human communities and leads to oppression and exploitation. The priority given in the Marxist theory to the rights to subsistence, work and social security is based on a conclusion about how social institutions must be organized to overcome this oppression. In this sense the Marxist approach to rights is strategic. It does not deny the significance and value of political liberty for all phases of history. Rather it judges that this liberty is subordinate to other human goods in the historical process which leads from capitalism to communism.

A strategic morality, as we are using the term, is a synthesis of historical interpretation and basic value commitments. It is more concrete and specific than what Daniel Callahan has called a "moral policy" because of its reliance on a particular reading of the social and historical data. Callahan defines a moral policy as "any culturally, philosophically or religiously chosen, given or accepted way of devising, relating and ordering moral rules . . . whatever the accepted method of ordering the rules might be." [3] In our context a moral policy would be a chosen, given or accepted way of ordering human rights. In Callahan's view, different moral policies can be equally compatible with the same reading of the scientific data on the human situations which they concern. A moral strategy, on the other hand, is dependent on a particular interpretation of the significance of these data. For this reason it seems appropriate to categorize the contemporary human rights debate as heavily strategic in nature. Disagreements are in large part the result of *divergent* historical readings of the mechanism of social and economic interaction. Both liberal and Marxist thought propose the "ordering" of human rights they do, largely because of their conclusions about how the social system works. Their disagreement is a reflection of their desire to propose normative priorities which are strategically relevant to the social system as they interpret it.

Recent Roman Catholic criticisms of liberalism and Marxism have been directed chiefly at the way their strategic concerns tend to be collapsed into normative theoretical descriptions of the full content of human dignity and human rights. When this happens strategic morality becomes ideology—a mode of thought which narrows its normative description of the human person in the interest of strategic action. Paul VI, for example, rejects both the liberal and the Marxist programs on the ground that

> the Christian who wishes to live his faith in a political activity which he thinks of as service cannot without contradicting himself adhere to ideological systems which radically or substantially go against his faith or his concept of man.[4]

The Catholic critique of these two contending approaches to the institutionalization of rights is aimed primarily at the narrowness of their normative "concepts of man."

Preoccupation with foundational questions is surely an appropriate response for a religious tradition whose fundamental concerns are the questions of the ultimate meaning and purpose of human existence. This preoccupation, however, has prevented the recent Catholic discussions of human rights from recognizing that not every strategic morality need be ideological in the negative sense. Paul VI has asserted that "Christian faith is above and is sometimes opposed to the ideologies."[5] The pope goes on to urge action and practical commitment in the political sphere. In his exhortation to action and commitment, however, he is reluctant to specify any coherent vision of strategic priorities. In his words:

> Going beyond every system, without however failing to commit himself concretely to serving his brothers, [the Christian] will assert, in the very midst of his options, the specific character of the Christian contribution for a positive transformation of society.[6]

The effort to stand "above ideology" and "beyond every system" has led to a loss of explicit strategic direction in recent Catholic theory.

It is not necessary, however, to abandon the effort to construct strategically useful moral norms in order to avoid an excessively narrow notion of human dignity. There is increasing evidence in analyses of social patterns which lead to the violation of human rights that ideological narrowness in the definition of rights is not only problematic from a normative and foundational point of view but is also strategically shortsighted. This evidence suggests that it should be possible to develop a set of relevant moral priorities for human rights claims which are not subject to normatively objectionable ideological narrowness.

Patricia Weiss Fagen of the Center for International Policy has noted that many countries which show a pattern of rights violations in the civil and political sphere also fail to meet the basic human needs of their citizens. Violations of civil and political rights increasingly appear to be linked with failure to respect social and economic rights.[7] Fagan notes, for example, that the present military government in Chile, in order to improve its access to credit with international financial institutions, such as the World Bank and the International Monetary Fund, has adopted an economic policy of curtailed government spending, reduced wages and general domestic austerity. As a result, real wages have fallen substantially, health conditions have deteriorated, and public health expenditures have been cut in half.[8] Similar pressures in the international credit and money markets led Argentina's military government to an austerity program which brought real wages to their lowest level in 30 years. Wage earners' share in the total national income has dropped to 31%, its lowest level since 1935. This phenomenon is not only visible in Latin America. In Portugal, efforts to implement policies which placed further burdens of national austerity on the poor in order to achieve economic stability led to the fall of that country's first elected government since 1932. Riots broke out when similar efforts were made in Egypt.

On the basis of data and analysis such as this it is not surprising that heavy restrictions in the area of civil and political rights have increasingly been the pattern in the less developed countries. As Fagan remarks, economic policies which fail to address the unmet basic needs of the poor "could not have been implemented without massive political repression."[9] J. P. Pronk, Minister for Development Cooperation in the Netherlands makes the same point:

> In Latin America and elsewhere we see in a dramatic way how people set about achieving social justice, how they need to exercise political freedoms to do this, and how they are oppressed and become the victims of inhuman tortures. The link between the different categories [of rights] is shown clearly not only in the preambles to treaties but also in the practical exercise of human rights."[10]

There appears, therefore, to be more of a causal linkage between economic deprivation and the denial of rights to political participation, freedom from arbitrary arrest and torture, freedom to organize labor unions etc., than the liberal ideology can account for. Recent efforts to include a human rights factor in U.S. foreign policy has been insufficiently sensitive to this linkage because of the liberal roots of the American understanding of rights.[11]

Conversely, regimes of both the left and the right which adopt authoritarian modes of political organization and which deny civil and political rights in order to fulfill their economic goals also appear strategically off-target. Marxist analysis seems insufficiently sensitive to the importance of political freedom in its own right to account for the persistence of political dissent in the Soviet Union. When decisions about social policy and the allocation of economic resources are in Andrei Sakharov's words, "reached in a closed circle of secret advisors and shadow cabinets" [12] it is not surprising that political dissent is vigorous. The fact that a government proclaims itself to be socialist—whether Marxist-Leninist or not—does not guarantee that its economic policies will in fact serve the needs of the people living under its regime. Indira Gandhi justified her declaration of a "state of emergency" in India on socialist and developmental grounds. Such an invocation of socialist values did not prevent the population of rural and urban India from perceiving her policies as a threat to their political *and* economic interests.[13] The economic distribution patterns in authoritarian Brazil also indicate the dangers present when political liberty is subordinated to a particular economic program. The lopsided distribution of the results of the Brazilian "economic miracle" is a result of the fact that the policies which guide the country's economic life have been formed by a narrow-based elite rather than by a popular national debate.[14] The point we are arguing has been well made by the Chilean bishops in their criticism of authoritarian strategies for development on *economic* grounds. Their words, which are applicable to authoritarian regimes of both the left and the right, highlight the fact that politics and the formation of economic policy are inseparable. Their statement is worth citing at length:

> To maintain that economic problems admit of only one correct solution is to impose the absolute dominion of science and scientific elites over the needs and demands of human responsibility. It is also to assure that such decisions

> are based solely on scientific reasons, that no dogmatic reasoning or selfish group-interest is operative in them. But that is not the case. Doctrinaire positions and selfish group-interests often profoundly affect such decisions, even though their influence may go unnoticed.
>
> In the name of basic human rights and the right of participation, the Church asks that the various economic options be submitted to open debate. . . . There is usually more wisdom to be found in the give-and-take between various points of view than in one which is asserted dogmatically and without competition.[15]

In some developing countries, then, there appears to be a causal link between denial of political liberty and the maintenance of economic distribution patterns which deny the poor the basic necessities of life. Recent past history of relations between whites and blacks in the United States gives similar evidence of a causal linkage between denial of the vote and legal due process and reinforcement of patterns of economic deprivation. The Marxist critique of the abstract political liberty of liberal thought is a telling one. Like authoritarian political programs of the right, however, Marxism-Leninism fails to grasp the crucial importance of the active exercise of concrete political responsibility. When economic life is increasingly planned and bureaucratized, political engagement by all is necessary if the economic claims of all are to be heard and respected.

In noting these examples our intention is not to present a detailed analysis of the causes and consequences of human rights violations in these countries. Such a project is most important, but it is beyond our scope here.[16] Neither is it our purpose to propose a human rights policy for Chile, Argentina, Portugal, India, the United States, or for any other nation. Rather, these brief examples are cited in order to lend plausibility to the suggestion that there is a way in which the Catholic insistence on an inclusive theory of the foundations and content of human rights can be relevant to policy formation. These examples imply that there are causal connections between denial of basic necessities, restrictions of political liberties and limitations of the patterns of relationship and association in many countries throughout the world. If this is the case then a moral perspective on human rights will be strategically relevant to the protection of human dignity to the extent that it takes these linkages into account. Ideologies such as liberalism, Marxism-Leninism, and the rightist forms of authoritarianism increasingly prevalent in the developing world will be inadequate not only in their normative foundations but also in their strategic implications. They are objectionable not simply from the viewpoint of ethics but also that of good policy. The presence of such causal interconnections would imply that some form of democratic socialism is not simply a refuge for democrats with scruples about the plight of the poor or for socialists who are queasy about the use of power and authority. Rather an approach to human rights which acknowledges claims based on need, claims to political liberty and claims to participation in the full range of social relationships will be structurally and strategically congruent with the present human situation. A defense of the full range of human rights need not be simply a normative argument on the level of ethical theory. It can be advanced in a way that is strategically relevant to the formation of human rights policy.

THE PRIMACY OF SOCIAL RIGHTS

The concluding section of Chapter Two has presented a schematic analysis of the human rights set forward in John XXIII's *Pacem in Terris*.[17] A renewed understanding of the strategic implications of the Catholic rights tradition can be formulated with the help of that analysis. It was pointed out that human rights claims can be differentiated in two ways. According to the first of these, rights claims are differentiated by distinguishing different dimensions or sectors of the human personality which must be respected if individuals are to live with dignity. These sectors include the bodily, political, economic, sexual, familial and religious dimensions of the human personality. There are legitimate rights claims in each of these sectors. The second mode of differentiating rights is based on the way these claims are mediated by patterns of social interaction and by the institutional structures of society. Some claims arise directly from the dignity of the individual person, such as the right to life, work, and self-determination. These are personal rights. Others are mediated by social interdependence, such as the right to adequate health care, decent working conditions, a just wage and political participation. These we have called social rights. Finally, other claims are formulated in explicitly institutional terms, such as the right to a system of social security, to fair labor practices, a just system of property distribution and to the juridical protection of self-determination and political participation. These we have called instrumental rights.

The lines of the contemporary debate over human rights policy are most often drawn in terms of the first of these approaches to the differentiation of rights. The argument is shaped in terms of a series of trade offs between one or more personal rights. Thus in formulating policy one is asked to choose between economic well-being and political liberty, or between the protection of life and health and the economic freedom of a market economy. The conflicts between claims are conflicts between the major sectors within which the dignity of individual persons is either realized or threatened.

As we have argued above, however, this way of drawing the issue is simplistic. There are interconnections between the various sectors of rights that make the issue quite different from a political vs. economic trade off. There are positive causal links between the sectors which cause them to reinforce as well as compete with each other. Under the conditions which actually prevail in many nations today, a failure to meet basic needs leads to increased political repression and decreased self-determination. Denial of political liberty, the right to association, and the freedom of workers to organize often leads to lopsided development and the denial of the rights to food, housing, health and work for large parts of the population. In other words, the real conflicts which must be addressed by human rights policy are not simple trade offs between different dimensions of the dignity of individual persons. A strategically relevant moral perspective on human rights policy must be concerned principally with the interconnections between different dimensions of respect for human dignity.

At the same time, however, such a perspective will fail to be a genuinely moral one if it focuses exclusively on the structures of the "mega-institutions" of government, the economy, culture, etc. These institutions are instrumental means for protecting persons in society. The structures and functions of these institutions are morally significant only to the extent that they promote or impede the realization of personal dignity in society. If a perspective on human rights policy subordinates concern for these effects to commitment to particular institutional forms it becomes an ideology rather than a strategic morality. The content of instrumental rights, therefore, must be determined by examining the ways large social institutions shape the actual relationships between persons and either support or threaten their dignity. If, as we are maintaining, political institutions affect economic, cultural religious and family life as well as the realm of politics more narrowly conceived, then a human rights policy must take this into account. Constitutional and juridical structures must be scrutinized from the viewpoint of economic rights and basic human needs. Similarly, the impact of economic structures and of the distribution of economic power on political participation, freedom of association and health care must also be assessed in formulating policy.

Thus in increasingly interdependent societies it is clear that a strategic moral perspective on human rights policy must recognize the primary importance of the full set of social rights for the protection of human dignity. The effective establishment of both personal and instrumental rights is central to any human rights policy. The issue, however, is not a matter of deciding which trade offs among personal rights are justified and appropriate. Nor is it primarily a matter of establishing a set of independent and discrete instrumental rights in political, economic, health, religious and familial sectors of institutional life. Neither of these approaches pays sufficient attention to the interconnections which actually exist between personal rights or to the multiple social impacts of large-scale institutions. These interconnections and multiple impacts only come into view when the whole set of social rights is made the focus of concern.

The strategically significant conflicts which must be addressed by human rights policy, therefore, are those which exist between social rights and individual claims on the one hand and between social rights and dominant institutional arrangements on the other. Human dignity will not be protected by shaping policies which protect the unimpeded maximal exercise of personal rights. Though policy must protect the personal rights of all, this does not mean that the exercise of these rights knows no moral bounds. At the same time, the moral legitimacy of political, economic and other large institutions must be measured against the norm of the full set of social rights, not just those in the political sector or just those concerned with material and economic goals. Instrumental rights such as those to social security, juridical protection of political participation and private property are not abstract absolutes. The rights to exercise political influence or to own property and accumulate wealth are limited by the impact which such activities have on all the social rights of other persons in the given historical situation. The strategically important conflicts, and therefore the morally strategic priorities for rights policy, cut across the lines which divide liberal democracy and Marxist-Leninist socialism. The issue is not "trade offs" between personal rights but rather the subordination of both personal and instrumental rights to the set of rights which mediate and guarantee human dignity socially.

Social rights are also of high strategic moral importance in contemporary societies because these societies are undergoing increasingly rapid change. Social rights are specifications of the conditions which make participation in the life of society possible. In changing societies, whether of the developed or developing world, human beings are continually under the threat of being left behind or put aside as new economic, cultural or political configurations evolve. Social rights, such as the rights to political participation, adequate food, health care, assembly, association, etc., identify kinds of social interaction which are essential to human dignity. Without these, persons can neither survive nor flourish. In rapidly changing societies large-scale social structures must be continually scrutinized to determine how they are promoting or impeding these crucial forms of participation. Similarly, personal rights claims will remain abstractions unless the concrete social conditions necessary for their realization are emphasized in the policy formation process. In stable societies where the institutions of political, economic and cultural life are fixed and where all persons have a humanly respectable place within these institutions, instrumental and personal rights provide the principle defenses for human dignity. In changing societies, however, where different patterns of economic and political life are in conflict and tension with each other, neither the individual nor the institutional perspectives provide adequate guidance for policy formation. The purpose of human rights policy is to shape both individual action and institutional structures in ways which make essential forms of social interaction possible for all. Thus social rights are of high strategic importance in changing societies.

In their 1977 pastoral statement on the "Christian Requirements of a Political Order" the National Conference of Brazilian Bishops strongly emphasized the strategic importance of the social conditions of participation. This statement contrasts the conditions of participation which we have called social rights with conditions of "marginalization"—the state of persons who are "kept outside" the ongoing life of society. The state of marginalization is described as one in which social rights are violated and denied:

> To be marginalized . . . is to receive an unjust salary. It is to be deprived of education, medical attention, and credit; it is to be hungry and live in sordid huts; it is to be deprived of land by inadequate, unjust agrarian structures.
>
> To be marginalized is above all, not to be able to free oneself from these situations. To be marginalized is not to be able to take part freely in the process of creativity which forges the original culture of a people. To be marginalized is not to have effective representation to make known one's needs and aspirations in decision-making centers; it is to be seen not as a subject of rights but as an object of favors granted in the measure necessary to reduce the militancy of the common people; it is to be manipulated by propaganda.
>
> To be marginalized is not to have a chance to participate. It is to be deprived of the recognition of the dignity which God has conferred upon man.[18]

In an unsystematic but vivid way, this statement points to the major conflict affecting the implementation of human rights in developing countries like Brazil—the conflict between social privilege and marginality.

The situation which provoked the Brazilian Bishop's statement is representative of that which prevails in an increasing number of poorer countries. Since 1964 Brazil has been ruled by a military regime which seized power when President Goulart began serious pursuit of a reform program that threatened upper class interests. Under the military, civil liberties have been restricted. The press is tightly censored. Labor unions are under heavy government control. Torture, summary imprisonment and assassination of opponents of the military have occurred with distressing frequency.[19] The exclusion of dissenting groups from participation in the political life of the country has been vigorous. The freedom of the working class and peasants to organize in a way that makes their claims effective has been severely restricted. At the same time, the rich have obtained an increasingly large share of the country's total income and the poor a decreasingly small share. Between 1960 and 1970 the top five percent of income earners increased their share of the total national income from 27.4 to 36.3 percent. During the same period the share of the lower 80 percent decreased from 45.5 to 36.8 percent. The real value of the Brazilian minimum wage during the period from 1966 to 1974 fell to 68.2 percent of its value during the period from 1954 to 1962.[20] This "redistribution of wealth" has occurred in spite of Brazil's economic boom. It has been possible because of the government's effective authoritarian control of both the political and economic spheres. The Brazilian case illustrates how conflict between privileged and marginalized groups is not confined to any one sector of personal rights. It is present in the areas of income, education, health, nutrition, housing, property, political representation, social organization and information. Political, economic, educational and other forms of privilege are interconnected. The corresponding forms of marginalization are similarly interlocking.

The interconnection between the different aspects of privilege and marginalization is also evident in the history of the relations between the races in the United States. Before the emancipation of slaves and the ratification of the 13th, 14th and 15th Amendments to the U.S. Constitution, blacks were forcefully deprived of their rights by a tightly interlocking system which was politically tyrannical, economically exploitative and culturally racist in its dealings with them. The struggle for the rights of blacks in the United States has pressed forward on many fronts: suffrage, employment, housing, education.[21] The effort to overcome slavery's legacy of extreme marginalization for blacks and privilege for whites has been simultaneously a political, economic and cultural task.

The continuing interconnection of the political, economic and racial/cultural factors of the "American dilemma" is evident in the most recent Supreme Court decision regarding the use of busing to bring about the integration of public schools, *Milliken v. Bradley*. In a series of decisions beginning with *Brown v. Board of Education* in 1954, the Court has been increasing its recognition for the need of affirmative government action to insure participation of blacks in an integrated school system.[22] In *Milliken v. Bradley* this process of development reached a "stopping point." [23] In previous school desegregation decisions the Court ruled that the "inherently unequal" nature of separate schools for the two races, the injustice of school board policies which aimed to keep schools racially segregated, and the inherent racial stigma implied by segregation all called for affirmative remedy. Thus busing children from their neighborhood schools in other neighborhoods within the school district was mandated in Charlotte-Mecklenberg, Denver, and Boston. The *Milliken v. Bradley* decision, however, concerned a desegregation plan which would have involved busing students across the district line between Detroit and its surrounding suburbs. Though the Court agreed that busing should take place *within* Detroit, it struck down the part of the plan which called for busing across urban/suburban district lines. By implication, the Court's decision suggested that respect for the boundaries separating school districts must take precedence over the kind of integration deemed mandatory within districts. Since school district lines are political as well as educational boundaries, the Court chose in effect to give greater weight to prevailing political structures than to the racial factors which led to busing orders in earlier cases.

The economic and cultural consequences of this choice are not insignificant. The racial patterns in the schools of the entire metropolitan area of Detroit and its suburbs remain similar to patterns judged unacceptable when they occur within districts. The crucial importance assigned to the urban/suburban boundaries by *Milliken v. Bradley* reinforces the economic barrier separating wealthy suburban districts from poor urban ones. As Owen Fiss has remarked:

> The *Milliken* limitation creates an insulated position for suburbanites. They are relieved of the burdens of integration, yet there is no rational basis for treating them differently than those who still remain within the school district. . . . One can justifiably insist that there be limits [to the extent of busing]. But it is hard to understand why the line should be the one the Supreme Court set in *Milliken*. . . . It is a line that limits the practical import of *Brown* and its progeny for the predominantly black urban systems and it is a line that creates all the wrong incentives—those hastening white flight to the suburbs.[24]

The "insulation" of suburbs from central cities which the *Milliken* decision supports is simultaneously political, economic and cultural.

The recent busing decisions are evidently highly complex issues. It is not our intent to analyze them to the extent demanded for the actual formation of policy. The Detroit desegregation decision is an especially vivid example, however, of the interconnection between the political, economic and cultural/racial factors of both privilege and marginalization in the United States. A human or civil rights policy for the internal life of the United States must take these interconnections into account. One-sided emphases on political liberties, economic needs or cultural/racial identity will lead to policies not strategically suited to the actual state of affairs.

We can conclude, therefore, that the strategic moral perspective on human rights policy will be one which challenges patterns of privilege and marginalization whether these be political, economic or cultural. Such a perspective is appropriate in both developing and developed countries. It is also called for in efforts to formulate human rights policies which address the relations between nations, for patterns of privilege and marginalization are even more evident here than in the cases we have mentioned. Adequate human rights policies must give priority to protecting the full set of social rights for all persons. It will accomplish this by limiting personal privilege and by structuring political, economic and cultural institutions in ways which open them to the participation of all.

THREE PRIORITY PRINCIPLES

Our analysis of *Pacem in Terris* suggested that the full set of social rights includes the following: the rights to food, clothing, shelter, rest and medical care, the right to political participation, the rights to nationality and to migrate, the rights of assembly and association, the rights of adequate working conditions and a just wage, the right to found a family or to live singly, the right to procreate, the right to profess religion privately and publicly, the rights to freedom of expression and to education. The strategic implications of the primacy of these rights in interdependent and changing societies is evident from the fact that they concern three basic forms of human interaction and interdependence. Several of the rights make it explicit that *basic human needs* can be met only in community. Food, housing, work and health, for example, are basic necessities for every person. These are social rights, however, because the fulfillment of these needs can only occur through participation in the economic and productive life of society. Several other social rights concern the exercise of personal *freedom* in interaction with others. Political participation and the public profession of religious belief are two ways that personal freedom is expressed and realized in society. A third group, including the rights to assemble, organize associations and to found a family, guarantee respect for those *relationships* which bind persons to each other. These rights provide societal support for the interpersonal and group bonds necessary for human dignity.

The three areas of need, freedom and relationship provide

the basis for several priority principles which supply strategic moral guidance for human rights policy. All persons have personal rights to the basic material necessities when society is capable of meeting these needs. All persons have personal rights to exercise their human freedom and form interpersonal and group relationships. As we have argued, however, patterns of marginalization and privilege often prevent some persons from experiencing these rights in highly interdependent and changing societies. Policy, therefore, must seek to counteract marginalization in each of the areas of need, freedom and relationship. Specifically, the societal effort to implement and institutionalize rights should adopt the following three strategic moral priorities:

1) The needs of the poor take priority over the wants of the rich.
2) The freedom of the dominated takes priority over the liberty of the powerful.
3) The participation of marginalized groups takes priority over the preservation of an order which excludes them.

These three principles, it should be quickly noted, are not policies.[25] They are normative ethical standards, not programs. They are, however, much more proximate to the actual decisions which must be made in forming policy than are the lists of human rights found in *Pacem in Terris* and the Universal Declaration. They provide a kind of guidance for the formation of policy which the lists of rights do not because they quite consciously acknowledge the fact of conflict between the claims which different persons make on the community.

All persons have material needs and wants which demand respect. All persons have basic rights to food, housing, health, work, etc. But in the actual pushing and shoving of economic life, the wants of some are gratified at the expense of the basic needs of others. A human rights policy, therefore, must do more than abstractly proclaim the rights of all persons to have their basic needs fulfilled. It must set out to counteract the privilege of the rich whenever this denies minimal necessities to the poor. Conflict between the needs of some and the wants of others, both within nations and across national boundaries, is one of the predominant characteristics of contemporary society. An adequate human rights policy cannot avoid this conflict if it is to be responsive to the actual situation. Therefore, a choice must be made between protecting privilege and guaranteeing minimum standards of living for all. The first principle states what that choice must be.

It is also true that all persons have a claim to a measure of freedom in their efforts to determine the direction and shape of their lives. Political self-determination, the power to pursue one's goals, the freedom to express oneself and to worship—these are rights for all. Again, however, the conflicts of society work more to the advantage of some than of others. Some people have vastly more political power and influence than others. Some have a much greater measure of freedom to conduct their lives according to their own goals and wishes while others are at the mercy of political, social and economic circumstances largely beyond their influence. In the extreme, this disproportionate distribution of social, political and economic freedom amounts to slavery for some members of society. In our world the patterns of domination of the basic freedoms of some by the economic, political and cultural power of others is evident. As the 1971 Synod put it:

> Even though it is not for us to elaborate a very profound analysis of the situation of the world, we have nevertheless been able to perceive the serious injustices which are building around the world of men a network of domination, oppression and abuses which stifle freedom and which keep the greater part of humanity from sharing in the buidling up of and enjoyment of a more just and more fraternal world.[26]

The liberty of the powerful is frequently in conflict with the right of the dominated to a measure of freedom. Again, a human rights policy must choose between these conflicting freedoms. The second principle indicates the choice between privileged liberty and basic freedom which must be at the heart of an adequate human rights policy.

Finally, all persons have rights to share in the interpersonal and group relationships which sustain a sense of human community and fraternity and which enable persons to pursue their goals in effective ways. Some of these relationships are highly personal and built on friendship, shared belief, and love, such as the family and the church. Others are functional and goal-oriented, such as professional and occupational groups. Still others, such as racial, ethnic and cultural groups, are the result of circumstances of birth. Participation in groups and relationships such as these is an essential condition for the preservation of personal agency, as the principle of subsidiarity suggests. In an increasingly technological and bureaucratic society, however, access to the benefits of association depends on membership in elite groups. For example, economic elites who control large corporations, and the intellectual elites who have major influence on the formation of policy, derive a kind of effective agency from their group memberships which is denied to persons excluded from these groups because of their race, educational level, cultural background, religion or nationality. A human rights policy must recognize the importance of group life by respecting the principle of subsidiarity, but must also recognize that membership in some groups carries serious social disadvantages while membership in others conveys disproportional advantage. The relationships between various social groups are not organically harmonious but conflictual. Thus an adequate human rights policy must choose between supporting the privileges bestowed on elites by the existing social order and seeking to increase the social, economic, cultural and political participation of marginalized groups. The third principle indicates the nature of this strategic moral choice.

These three priority principles all rest on the acknowledgement of the reality of conflict between the claims of persons and groups in society. With the whole Catholic tradition, they recognize that all persons have justified claims corresponding to each of the basic dimensions of human dignity. Every human being possesses personal rights to the fulfillment of basic needs, the exercise of freedom and social participation mediated through interpersonal and group relationships. But these claims are not unlimited. The choices which must be made in formulating policy will be moral ones to the extent that they are an exercise of political solidarity. The conflicts between claims call for strategic action which will limit the claims of the privileged and expand the participation of the marginalized. Such action will itself involve conflict—it is political. At the same time, however, it is an expression of the bonds of solidarity which link persons to each other in a moral community. This kind of strategic action is an expression of Christian love. It is the principal strategic implication of a Christian understanding of human rights.

The strategic morality expressed in these three principles is both an expression and a renewal of the Catholic human rights tradition. These priorities are implicit in the most recent Roman Catholic social teachings, but they are present there in an undeveloped form. We propose these priorities as an intellectual and practical challenge both to the Catholic community and to the other participants in the human rights debate. They are an attempt to give recent developments in the Catholic rights tradition a solid theoretical base. Whether they are in fact strategically suited to the formation of policy in a pluralistic and conflicted world can finally be determined only by the test of action.

NOTES

1. Two studies by my colleague Brian H. Smith, S.J. indicate the many levels of conflict in which the Church is currently involved in Latin America. See his "Religion and Social Change: Classical Theories and New Formulations in the Context of Recent Developments in Latin America," *Latin American Research Review* 10, No. 2 (1975), pp. 3-34, and *The Political Role of the Chilean Catholic Church, 1925-1978.* (Forthcoming).

2. For a perceptive study of the consequences of the absence of an adequate theory of how conflicting claims should be dealt with, see Michael Howard Fleet, "Ideological Tendencies Within Chilean Christian Democracy," (Ph.D. dissertation, University of California at Los Angeles, 1971), Chap. 4.

3. Daniel Callahan, *Abortion: Law, Choice and Morality* (New York: MacMillan, 1970), p. 341-342.

4. *OA*, no. 26.

5. *OA*, no. 27.

6. *OA*, no. 36.

7. Patricia Weiss Fagan, "The Links Between Human Rights and Basic Needs," *Background* (Center for International Policy), Spring, 1978, p. 4.

8. Ibid., pp. 9 & 10. See also Brian H. Smith, S.J., "Silent Hunger in Chile," *America,* 132 (May 24, 1975), pp. 394-396.

9. Fagan, "The Links Between Human Rights and Basic Needs," p. 10.

10. J. P. Pronk, "Human Rights and Development Aid," *International Commission of Jurists Review* 18 (June, 1977), pp. 35-36.

11. Sandra Vogelgesang, "What Price Principle? U.S. Policy on Human Rights," *Foreign Affairs* (July, 1978), pp. 819-841.

12. Andrei Sakharov, *Progress, Coexistence and Intellectual Freedom,* pp. 61-62.

13. See the in-depth analysis by Francine R. Frankel, "Compulsion and Social Change: Is Authoritarianism the Solution to India's Economic Development Problems?" *World Politics* XXX (1978), pp. 215-240.

14. Kenneth S. Mericle, "Corporatist Control of the Working Class: Authoritarian Brazil Since 1964," in James M. Malloy, ed., *Authoritarianism and Corporatism in Latin America,* p. 306 and *passim.*

15. The Permanent Committee of the Chilean Episcopal Conference. "Our Life as a Nation," Pastoral Letter issued March 25, 1977, trans. from *El Mercurio,* Chile, March 26, 1977 by Orbis Books in *Latin American Bishops Discuss Human Rights* LADOC "Keyhole" Series, no. 15 (Washington, D.C.: 1977, Latin American Documentation), p. 53.

16. This book is part of a larger project being conducted by the Woodstock Theological Center. The Center's project on "Human Rights, Needs and Power in an Interdependent World" is investigating these larger questions in a more systematic way. I believe that the Center's study will validate the conclusions drawn on somewhat impressionistic grounds in what follows. Until the completion of that study the strategic priorities presented here may be considered as a theses needing further proof. The results of the Center's work, so far however, suggest that they are more than mere hypotheses.

17. See Figure 1, p. 98 above.

18. The National Conference of Brazilian Bishops, "Christian Requirements of a Political Order," in *Latin American Bishops Discuss Human Rights,* LADOC "Keyhole" Series, no. 16, pp. 60-61.

19. In 1975, Amnesty International reached the following conclusion about the situation in Brazil: "We can say that torture is widespread and that it can be said to constitute administrative practice. It appears to be used in the majority of interrogations, even against people detained for a short period of time or 'rounded up' in 'sweep' arrests and held because they lack the necessary identification papers. Motives appear to be the extraction of information and confessions, and intimidation of potential dissidents. Though it has often been claimed that torture takes place under the least stable regimes, the recent escalation of torture in Brazil appears to belie this; the systematization of torture seems to reflect

the Brazilian authorities' desire to quell what they see as a constant threat from international and internal 'subversion.' " Amnesty International, *Report on Torture* (New York: Farrar, Straus and Giroux, 1975), p. 199.

20. Mericle, "Corporatist Control of the Working Class," pp. 303-338.

21. The literature on the struggle, of course, is vast. See, for example, Louis H. Pollak, "Emancipation and Law: A Century of Progress," in Robert A. Goldwin, ed., *100 Years of Emancipation* (Chicago: Rand McNally, 1969), pp. 158-181.

22. For a trenchant analysis of these developments, see Archibald Cox, *The Role of the Supreme Court in American Government* (New York: Oxford University Press, 1976), chap. IV, "The Affirmative Duties of Government."

23. Owen M. Fiss, "School Desegregation: The Uncertain Path of Law," in M. Cohen, T. Nagel and T. Scanlon, eds., *Equality and Preferential Treatment* (Princeton: Princeton University Press, 1977), p. 183.

24. Fiss, "School Desegregation," pp. 186, 190.

25. The notion of strategic priority principles used here is similar to what J. H. Oldham and John Coleman Bennet have called "Middle axioms" and to Paul Ramsey's notion of "decision and action-oriented" teachings which provide direction for policy. See John Bennet, *Christian Ethics and Social Policy* (New York: Scribner's, 1953), p. 79 and Paul Ramsey, *Who Speaks for the Church?* (Nashville: Abingdon, 1967), pp. 16-17. I prefer to use the formulations "strategic moral priorities" in order to indicate both the presence of conflict and the need for change which lie at the basis of these principles.

26. *JW,* no. 3.

ABBREVIATIONS

The following abbreviations for official documents of the Roman Catholic Church are used in the notes which follow. Citations are from the translations noted here. Bibliographical information on the translations employed for all documents is included here for easy reference. It should be noted that not all English translations of individual documents adopt the same scheme of paragraph numbering. The translations used here have been chosen for their accuracy and availability.

AA *Apostolicam Actuositatem.* Decree on the Apostolate of the Laity of Vatican II. In Walter M. Abbott, S.J. and Msgr. Joseph Gallagher, eds., *The Documents of Vatican II,* pp. 489-521.

AP *Aeterni Patris.* 1879 Encyclical of Leo XIII on Christian Philosophy. In Etienne Gilson, ed., *The Church Speaks to the Modern World: The Social Teachings of Leo XIII* (Garden City, N.Y.: Doubleday, Image, 1954), pp. 31–54.

Arc *Arcanum.* 1880 Encyclical of Leo XIII on Christian Marriage. In Gilson, pp. 88-113.

CC *Casti Connubii.* 1930 Encyclical of Pius XI on Christian Marriage. In Joseph Husslein, S.J., *Social Wellsprings, Vol. II. Eighteen Encyclicals of Social Reconstruction by Pope Pius XI* (Milwaukee: Bruce, 1942), pp. 125-173.

CCC *Caritate Christi Compulsi.* 1932 Encyclical of Pius XI on the Sacred Heart Devotion. In Husslein, vol. II, pp. 262-277.

DH *Dignitatis Humanae.* Declaration on Religious Freedom of Vatican II. In Abbott and Gallagher, pp. 675-696.

DIM *Divini Illius Magistri.* 1929 Encyclical of Pius XI on Christian Education. In Husslein, vol. II, pp. 89-121.

Diut *Diuturnum.* 1881 Encyclical of Leo XIII on Civil Government. In Gilson, pp. 141-156.

DR *Divini Redemptoris*. 1937 Encyclical of Pius XI on Atheistic Communism. In Husslein, vol. II, pp. 341-374.

FC *Firmissimam Constantiam*. 1937 Encyclical of Pius XI on Catholic Action in Mexico. In Husslein, vol. II, pp. 376-390.

GC *Graves de Communi*. 1901 Encyclical of Leo XIII on Christan Democracy. In Gilson, pp. 315-330.

GS *Gaudium et Spes*. Pastoral Constitution on the Church in the Modern World of Vatican II. In Abbott and Gallagher, pp. 199-308.

HG *Humanum Genus*. 1884 Encyclical of Leo XIII on Freemasonry. In Gilson, pp. 117-139.

HV *Humanae Vitae*. 1968 Encyclical of Paul VI on the Regulation of Birth. In Joseph Gremillion, ed., *The Gospel of Peace and Justice: Catholic Social Teaching since Pope John* (Maryknoll, N.Y.: Orbis, 1976), pp. 427-444.

ID *Immortale Dei*. 1885 Encyclical of Leo XIII on th Christian Constitution of States. In Gilson, pp. 161-187.

IP *In Plurimis*. 1888 Encyclical of Leo XIII on the Abolition of Slavery. In Gilson, pp. 293-312.

JW *Justice in the World*. Document issued by the 1971 Synod of Bishops. In Gremillion, pp. 513-529.

LG *Lumen Gentium*. Dogmatic Constitution on the Church of Vatican II. In Abbott and Gallagher, pp. 14-101.

Lib *Libertas*. 1888 Encyclical of Leo XIII on Human Liberty. In Gilson, pp. 57-85.

MBS *Mit Brennender Sorge*. 1937 Encyclical of Pius XI on the position of the Church in Germany. In Husslein, vol. II, pp. 318-338.

MM *Mater et Magistra*. 1961 Encyclical of John XXIII on the Church and Social Progress. In Gremillion, pp. 143-200.

NA *Nostra Aetate*. Declaration of Vatican II on the Relationship of the Church to Non-Christian Religions. In Abbott and Gallagher, pp. 660–668.

NAB *Non Abbiamo Bisogno*. 1931 Encyclical of Pius XI on Catholic Action. In Husslein, vol. II, pp. 235-260.

OA *Octogesima Adveniens*. 1971 Apostolic Letter of Paul VI on the Church and Political Activity. In Gremillion, pp. 477-512.

PP *Populorum Progressio*. 1967 Encyclical of Paul VI on the Development of Peoples. In Gremillion, pp. 387-415.

PT *Pacem in Terris*. 1963 Encyclical of John XXIII on World Peace. In Gremillion, pp. 201-241.

QA *Quadragesimo Anno*. 1931 Encyclical of Pius XI on the Reconstruction of the Social Order. In Husslein, vol. II, 178-234.

QAM *Quod Apostolici Muneris*. 1878 Encyclical of Leo XIII on *Socialism*. In Gilson, pp. 189-199.

QP *Quas Primas*. 1925 Encyclical of Pius XI on the Kingship of Christ. In Husslein, vol. II, pp. 30-46.

RN *Rerum Novarum*. 1891 Encyclical of Leo XIII on the Rights and Duties of Capital and Labor. In Gilson, pp. 205-244.

SC *Sapientiae Christianae*. 1890 Encyclical of Leo XIII on Christian Citizenship. In Gilson, pp. 248-275.

SP *Summi Pontificatus*. 1939 Encyclical of Pius XII on the Function of the State in the Modern World. Washington, D.C.: National Catholic Welfare Conference, 1939.

UA *Ubi Arcano*. 1922 Encyclical of Pius XI on the Peace of Christ in the Reign of Christ. In Husslein, vol. II, pp. 5-26.

Index